SPANISH
by ASSOCIATION

The Linkword Language System

*A Proven Technique for Learning . . . and Remembering . . .
Basic Spanish Vocabulary & Grammar*

Dr. Michael M. Gruneberg

New York Chicago San Francisco Lisbon London Madrid Mexico City
Milan New Delhi San Juan Seoul Singapore Sydney Toronto

21DIG/DIG 15

ISBN-13: 978-0-8442-9447-6
ISBN-10:   0-8442-9447-0
Library of Congress Control Number: 2004113596

Cover design by Nick Panos

McGraw-Hill books are available at special quantity discounts to use as premiums and sales promotions, or for use in corporate training programs. For more information, please write to the Director of Special Sales, Professional Publishing, McGraw-Hill, Two Penn Plaza, New York, NY 10121-2298. Or contact your local bookstore.

This book is printed on acid-free paper.

CONTENTS

SECTION 7

SECTION 8

SECTION 9

SECTION 10

FOREWORD

Anyone reading a book that teaches a foreign language might well
wonder why it has been written by a memory expert and not a linguist or
a language teacher. Well, the simple fact is that if you want to *remember*
what you are taught, then putting ease of remembering at the center of
the design of the book is likely to lead to far higher levels of learning
than a book written only with the ideas of a linguist in mind. Of course,
this book has been written by a memory expert working with skilled
linguists so that the language aspects are correct.

The basic "memory idea" of the book to help you remember what you
are taught is the "method of association," or the linkword method.
Learning a foreign language is all about associating what you are familiar
with, e.g., the word *bread,* with something you are not familiar with—
the word for *bread* is *pan* in Spanish or Japanese. There are two possible
ways you can do this. You can repeat the words *bread* and *pan* together
until you are sure it sticks, or you can "picture" yourself putting some
bread into a pan. This picturing technique is known as the method of
association, or the linkword method. Of course, as far as learning foreign
language vocabulary is concerned, there is a further complication that the
foreign word may not sound like *any* English word. For example, the
Spanish for *cow* is *vaca,* which sounds like "vaka." What you do in this
situation is to imagine a *cow* with a *vacuum* cleaner, cleaning a field. The
linkword *vacuum* does not have to be identical to the foreign word in
order to be able to associate *cow* with "vaka" through the use of mental
pictures. It may sound bizarre, but over fifty studies published in
scientific journals have found this technique to materially increase the
level of foreign vocabulary learning. In one study of Spanish, for
example, learning increased from 28% for rote learning to 88% using
the picture association technique.

The method of association was known to the Greeks as an efficient way
of improving memory, and the application of the method of association
to learning foreign languages was discussed as long ago as the nineteenth

v

century. It is only recently, however, that psychologists have shown how effective the method is when applied to learning foreign language vocabulary, and the present book is, as far as the author is aware, the first to make use of the method to provide a whole course for foreign language learners, teaching not only an extensive vocabulary but providing a basic grammar and using sentence examples.

The course consists of hundreds of useful words that, with the grammar provided, can be strung together to form sentences. In eight to twelve hours, you should be able to go right through the course and acquire enough useful knowledge to communicate when you go abroad.

The author has published a number of studies* of the courses that show how fast and easy people find it. In one study of travel executives, the group was taught Spanish for *twelve* contact hours. They were then tested by an independent test expert who found they were virtually errorless on the four hundred word vocabulary and grammar they had been taught. The independent expert estimated they would normally have taken *forty* hours to reach that standard. In a second study, a group of bankers was taught a vocabulary of at least six hundred words and basic grammar in four days. However, it is not just the linguistically able who benefit from the courses. In one study, thirteen-year-old low-ability language students were given one session every week using the Spanish by Association course and another session using conventional teaching methods for one term. At the end of the term, the students were given a test where the mean vocabulary score on Spanish following con-ventional teaching was 23.75% compared to 69% for the Spanish by Association course. One student out of sixteen passed with conventional teaching, fourteen out of sixteen passed with Spanish by Association teaching. The studies carried out to date show that the courses are ideal for anyone who wants to learn the basics of a language in a hurry, whether for travel, for business, or for schoolwork. For many people such as the tourist who just wants to get by or the business person who has to be in Berlin next Wednesday, then Paris next Friday, their language needs do not involve the mastery of a single language in depth but the rapid acquisition of a basic language to get by with. Because they are designed specifically to enhance speed and ease of language acquisition and to help

*M. M. Gruneberg and G. C. Jacobs (1991), "In Defence of Linkword," *The Language Learning Journal* (3), 25–29.

you remember what you have learned, the By Association courses are uniquely suited to meet such needs, as well as the needs of those who might have experienced language learning difficulties earlier in life.

INTRODUCTION

WHO IS *SPANISH BY ASSOCIATION* FOR?

The short answer is that By Association books are for anyone and everyone who wants to learn the basics of a language in a hurry. It can be used by children or by adults. Even young children who cannot read can be taught Spanish words by a parent reading out the images.

The By Association courses have been carefully designed to teach you a basic grammar and words in a simple step-by-step way that anyone can follow. After about ten to twelve hours, or even less, you will have a vocabulary of literally hundreds of words and the ability to string these words together to form sentences. The course is ideal, therefore, for the tourist or business person who just wants the basics in a hurry so he or she can be understood, e.g., in the hotel, arriving at the destination, sightseeing, eating out, in emergencies, telling the time and so on.

The course is also an ideal supplement to schoolwork. Many students feel that they remember words for the first time when introduced to the By Association system, and understand basic grammar for the first time too!

HOW TO USE *SPANISH BY ASSOCIATION*

1. You will be presented with words like this:
   The Spanish for **rice** is **arroz**.
   Imagine someone shooting **arrows** at your plate of rice.
   What you do is to imagine this picture in your mind's eye as vividly as possible.

2. After you have read the image for a word, you should visualize it in your mind's eye for about ten seconds before moving on to the next word. If you do not spend enough time thinking about the image, it will not stick in your memory as well as it should.

3. Sometimes the word in Spanish and in English is the same or very similar. For example, the word for **taxi** in Spanish is **taxi**. When this happens, you will be asked to associate the word in some way with a bullfighter.

   Imagine a taxi filled with bullfighters. Whenever bullfighters come to mind, therefore, you will know the word is the same or similar in English and Spanish.

4. The examples given in the course may well strike you as silly and bizarre. They have deliberately been designed in this way to show up points of grammar and to get away from the idea that you should remember useful phrases "parrot fashion."

5. **Accents**
   When you see this accent ñ, you should pronounce it NYUH.
   For example: The Spanish for **tomorrow** is **mañana**.
   MANYANA is the way the word is pronounced.

   When you see an acute accent (´) on a vowel, you should emphasize the syllable with the accented vowel in it.

2

For example: The Spanish for **mouse** is **ratón.**
RAT *ON* is the way the word is pronounced (*not RAT* ON).

6. **Pronunciation**

The approximate pronunciation of words is given in parentheses after the word is presented for the first time.
For example: The Spanish for **cow** is **vaca** (VAKA).
(VAKA) is the way the word is pronounced.

Do not worry too much about these pronunciations to begin with. The approximate pronunciation given in parentheses will allow you to be understood.

SOME USEFUL HINTS

1. It is usually best to go through the course as quickly as possible. Many people can get through most of the course in a weekend, especially if they start on Friday evening.

2. Take a break of about ten minutes between each section, and always *stop* if you feel tired.

3. Don't worry about forgetting a few words, and do not go back to relearn words you have forgotten. Just think of how much you are learning, and try to pick up the forgotten words when it comes time to review.

4. Review after Section 4, Section 8 and at the end of the course. Then review the whole course a week later and a month later.

5. Don't worry if you forget some of the words or grammar after a time. Relearning is extremely fast, and going through the book for a few hours just before you go abroad will quickly get you back to where you were.

6. The course will not give you conversational fluency. You can't expect this until you go abroad and live in a country for a period of time. What it will give you very rapidly is the ability to survive in a large number of situations you will meet abroad. Once you have gotten this framework, you will find it much easier to pick up more words and grammar when you travel.

IMPORTANT NOTE

The first section of the course can be basically regarded as a training section designed to get you into the By Association method quickly and easily.

After about forty-five minutes, you will have a vocabulary of about thirty words and be able to translate sentences. Once you have finished Section 1, you will have the confidence to go through the rest of the course just as quickly. Animal words are used in the first section since they are a large group of "easy to image" words. Many animal words of course are useful to have as they are often met abroad, e.g., dog, cat, etc., or they are edible!

Finally, when it comes to translating sentences, the answers are given at the bottom of the page. You may find it useful to cover up the answers before you try to do the translations.

SECTION 1

ANIMALS

☐ **Think of each image in your mind's eye for about ten seconds.**
For example, the Spanish for **cow** is **vaca**. Imagine in your mind's eye for ten seconds a cow with a **vacuum** cleaner cleaning a field.

☐ *Note: The word on the right-hand side of the page (IN PARENTHESES) is the way the word is pronounced.*

SOME ANIMALS

* The Spanish for **cat** is **gato**.   (GATO)
  Imagine you **get to** hold a lovely cat.

* The Spanish for **dog** is **perro**.   (PERRO)
  Imagine a dog **pirouetting**.

* The Spanish for **goat** is **cabra**.   (KABRA)
  Imagine a **cobra** striking at a goat, perhaps at
  its beard.

* The Spanish for **bull** is **toro**.   (TORO)
  Imagine a **toreador** fighting a bull.

* The Spanish for **cow** is **vaca**.   (VAKA)
  Imagine a cow with a **vacuum** cleaner cleaning the field.

* The Spanish for **duck** is **pato**.   (PATO)
  Imagine **patting** a duck on its head, or imagine
  duck paté.

* The Spanish for **goose** is **ganso**.   (GANSO)
  Imagine **gangs of** geese going around together.

* The Spanish for **pig** is **puerco**.   (POO ERKO)
  Imagine eating **pork** straight from a pig.

* The Spanish for **donkey** is **burro**.   (BOORRO)
  Imagine a donkey at a writing **bureau**.

* The Spanish for **frog** is **rana**.   (RANA)
  Imagine you **ran a** mile after seeing a horrible frog.

7

- What is the English for **rana**? ——————

- What is the English for **burro**? ——————

- What is the English for **puerco**? ——————

- What is the English for **ganso**? ——————

- What is the English for **pato**? ——————

- What is the English for **vaca**? ——————

- What is the English for **toro**? ——————

- What is the English for **cabra**? ——————

- What is the English for **perro**? ——————

- What is the English for **gato**? ——————

← *Look back for the answers*

☐ *You can write your answers in*

- What is the Spanish for **frog**? _____

- What is the Spanish for **donkey**? _____

- What is the Spanish for **pig**? _____

- What is the Spanish for **goose**? _____

- What is the Spanish for **duck**? _____

- What is the Spanish for **cow**? _____

- What is the Spanish for **bull**? _____

- What is the Spanish for **goat**? _____

- What is the Spanish for **dog**? _____

- What is the Spanish for **cat**? _____

← *Look back for the answers*

ELEMENTARY GRAMMAR

The first bit of grammar to learn is that all nouns (persons, animals, things), whether living or nonliving, are either masculine or feminine. If they end in an *o*, they are masculine.

➜ *For example,*

- *Bull* is *toro*, *cat* is *gato*, and *dog* is *perro*. All these words end in an *o* and are therefore masculine words.

Words that end in an *a* are feminine words. *Cabra* for *goat* and *vaca* for *cow* end in an *a* and are therefore feminine words.

□ **Tell the genders of these words:**

- vaca

- pato

- burro

- rana

- ganso

□ *The answers are:*

- *vaca* is *feminine*

- *pato* is *masculine*

- *burro* is *masculine*

- *rana* is *feminine*

- *ganso* is *masculine*

A few words do not end in *o* or *a*. Do not worry about these for now. We will deal with them later.

MORE ANIMALS

☐ **Think of each image in your mind's eye for about ten seconds**

- The Spanish for **monkey** is **mono**.   (MONO)
  Imagine a monkey wearing a **monocle**.

- The Spanish for **rat** is **rata**.   (RATA)
  Imagine a **rat** fighting a bullfighter.

- The Spanish for **mouse** is **ratón**.   (RATON)
  Imagine a **rat on** a mouse, squashing it flat.

- The Spanish for **animal** is **animal**.   (ANEEMAL)
  Imagine a bullfighter surrounded by a whole lot
  of different **animals**.

- The Spanish for **salmon** is **salmón**.   (SALMON)
  Imagine a **salmon** leaping over a bullfighter.

- The Spanish for **wasp** is **avispa**.   (AVEESPA)
  Imagine **a whisper** in your ear as a wasp buzzes
  near you.

- The Spanish for **bear** is **oso**.   (OSO)
  Imagine a big grizzly bear **oh so** near you.

- The Spanish for a (live) **fish** is **pez**.   (PES)
  Imagine a fish **pacing** up and down in an
  aquarium.

- The Spanish for **bee** is **abeja**.   (ABEHA)
  Imagine **a baker** being chased by a bee.

13

☐ *You can write your answers in*

- What is the English for **abeja**? _____

- What is the English for **pez**? _____

- What is the English for **oso**? _____

- What is the English for **avispa**? _____

- What is the English for **salmón**? _____

- What is the English for **animal**? _____

- What is the English for **ratón**? _____

- What is the English for **rata**? _____

- What is the English for **mono**? _____

← *Look back for the answers*

☐ *You can write your answers in*

- What is the Spanish for **bee**? _____

- What is the Spanish for **fish**? _____

- What is the Spanish for **bear**? _____

- What is the Spanish for **wasp**? _____

- What is the Spanish for **salmon**? _____

- What is the Spanish for **animal**? _____

- What is the Spanish for **mouse**? _____

- What is the Spanish for **rat**? _____

- What is the Spanish for **monkey**? _____

← *Look back for the answers*

ELEMENTARY GRAMMAR

You learned after the last group of words that all nouns are either masculine or feminine. If they end in *o*, they are masculine, like *gato* for *cat*. If they end in *a*, they are feminine, like *cabra* for *goat*.

If they do not end in either an *o* or an *a*, you can assume they are masculine, although you will make the occasional mistake.

☐ If the word is *masculine*, then the word for *the* is *el*.

➜ *So,*

- *el toro* is *the bull*

- *el gato* is *the cat*

- *el mono* is *the monkey*

Try to remember that men are *hell* to live with.

☐ If the word is *feminine*, however, then the word for *the* is *la*.

➜ *So,*

- *la vaca* is *the cow*

- *la rata* is *the rat*

- *la cabra* is *the goat*

As we saw just now, where the word does not end in an *a* or an *o*, such as *animal, ratón, pez,* etc., it is almost always masculine.

➜ *So,*

- *el animal* is *the animal*

- *el pez* is *the fish*

☐ **Now cover up the answers below and translate the following:**

- the dog
- the salmon
- the goat
- the cow
- the bee
- the wasp

- the mouse
- the animal
- the donkey
- the duck
- the frog
- the bear

☐ *The answers are:*

- el perro
- el salmón
- la cabra
- la vaca
- la abeja
- la avispa

- el ratón
- el animal
- el burro
- el pato
- la rana
- el oso

SOME ADJECTIVES (DESCRIPTIVE WORDS)

☐ **Think of each image in your mind's eye for about ten seconds**

- The Spanish for **hard** is **duro**.   (DOORO)
  Imagine something hard and **durable**.

- The Spanish for **quick** is **rápido**.   (RAPEEDO)
  Imagine something **rapid** and quick.

- The Spanish for **quiet** is **tranquilo**.   (TRANKEELO)
  Imagine everything being **tranquil** and quiet.

- The Spanish for **fresh** is **fresco**.   (FRESKO)
  Imagine seeing a **fresco** freshly painted on a
  wall.

- The Spanish for **good** is **bueno**.   (BOO ENO)
  Imagine there must be something good in
  buenos Aires!

- The Spanish for **bad** is **malo**.   (MALO)
  Imagine a bad marsh**mallo**w.

19

☐ *You can write your answers in*

- What is the English for **malo**?   _____

- What is the English for **bueno**?   _____

- What is the English for **fresco**?   _____

- What is the English for **tranquilo**?   _____

- What is the English for **rápido**?   _____

- What is the English for **duro**?   _____

← *Look back for the answers*

20

☐ *You can write your answers in*

- What is the Spanish for **bad**? _____

- What is the Spanish for **good**? _____

- What is the Spanish for **fresh**? _____

- What is the Spanish for **quiet**? _____

- What is the Spanish for **quick**? _____

- What is the Spanish for **hard**? _____

← *Look back for the answers*

21

ELEMENTARY GRAMMAR

The Spanish word for *is* is *está*.

Imagine *a star* is born.

➡ *For example:*

- *the pig is* is *el puerco está*

- *the dog is* is *el perro está*

To say *the pig is quick,* you simply say:

El puerco está rápido

- *The dog is quick* is *El perro está rápido*

If the noun is feminine, such as *la vaca, la cabra,* and so on, then the ending of the adjective changes to an *a* from an *o* to agree with the noun.

➡ *So,*

- *The cow is quick* is *La vaca está rápida* (Note: Not *rápido*)

➡ *Similarly,*

- *The goat is quick* is *La cabra está rápida*

☐ **Now cover up the answers below and translate the following:**

☐ *(You can write your answers in)*

1. The dog is fresh.

2. The fish is quick.

3. The cat is fresh.

4. The goat is quiet.

5. The cow is quick.

_____

_____

_____

_____

_____

_____

☐ *The answers are:*

1. El perro está fresco.
2. El pez está rápido.
3. El gato está fresco.
4. La cabra está tranquila.
5. La vaca está rápida.

The other adjectives (descriptive words) you have learned can be used in the same way, but exactly how they should be used will be explained in the next section.

☐ **Now cover up the answers below and translate the following:**

☐ *(You can write your answers in)*

1. El animal está fresco.

2. El oso está rápido.

3. El ganso está tranquilo.

4. El mono está fresco.

5. La avispa está rápida.

_____

_____

_____

_____

_____

_____

_____

☐ *The answers are:*

1. The animal is fresh.

2. The bear is quick.

3. The goose is quiet.

4. The monkey is fresh.

5. The wasp is quick.

SOME USEFUL ANIMAL WORDS

☐ **Think of each image in your mind's eye for about ten seconds**

- The Spanish for **bird** is **pájaro.**   (PAHARO)
  Imagine a **parrot** chasing a bird.

- The Spanish for **horse** is **caballo.**   (KABALYO)
  Imagine saying, "I'll **cable you** if my horse
  wins."

- The Spanish for **jellyfish** is **medusa.**   (MEDOOSA)
  Imagine seeing **Medusa** with her head of
  snakes, but when you look carefully, it is a
  jellyfish.

- The Spanish for **fly** is **mosca.**   (MOSKA)
  Imagine **Moscow** invaded by a cloud of flies.

- The Spanish for **chicken** is **pollo.**   (POLYO)
  Imagine getting a chicken to **pull you** along.

☐ *You can write your answers in*

- What is the English for **pollo**? _____

- What is the English for **mosca**? _____

- What is the English for **medusa**? _____

- What is the English for **caballo**? _____

- What is the English for **pájaro**? _____

← *Look back for the answers*

☐ *You can write your answers in*

- What is the Spanish for **chicken**? _____

- What is the Spanish for **fly**? _____

- What is the Spanish for **jellyfish**? _____

- What is the Spanish for **horse**? _____

- What is the Spanish for **bird**? _____

← *Look back for the answers*

ELEMENTARY GRAMMAR

When you have a noun and an adjective together like *hard pig*, *quiet cow*, or *quick bear*, then the adjective usually comes after the noun.

➜ *For example:*

- *the quiet bee* is *la abeja tranquila*

- *the hard pig* is *el puerco duro*

- *the quick frog* is *la rana rápida*

☐ **Now cover up the answers below and translate the following:**

☐ *(You can write your answers in)*

1. The quick cat is quiet.

2. The hard pig is quick.

3. The fresh bird is quick.

4. The quiet jellyfish is quick.

5. The quick horse is fresh.

_____

_____

_____

_____

_____

_____

_____

☐ *The answers are:*

1. El gato rápido está tranquilo.

2. El puerco duro está rápido.

3. El pájaro fresco está rápido.

4. La medusa tranquila está rápida.

5. El caballo rápido está fresco.

☐ **Now cover up the answers below and translate the following:**

☐ *(You can write your answers in)*

1. El pollo tranquilo está fresco.

2. La rana fresca está rápida.

3. La mosca rápida está tranquila.

4. El pollo fresco está rápido.

5. La medusa fresca está rápida.

_____

_____

_____

_____

_____

_____

_____

_____

☐ *The answers are:*

1. The quiet chicken is fresh.

2. The fresh frog is quick.

3. The quick fly is quiet.

4. The fresh chicken is quick.

5. The fresh jellyfish is quick.

IMPORTANT NOTE

Some of the sentences in this course might strike you as being a bit odd!

However, they have been carefully constructed to make you think much more about what you are translating. This helps the memory process and gets away from the idea of learning useful phrases "parrot fashion."

But of course, having learned with the help of these seemingly odd sentences, you can easily construct your own sentences to suit your particular needs.

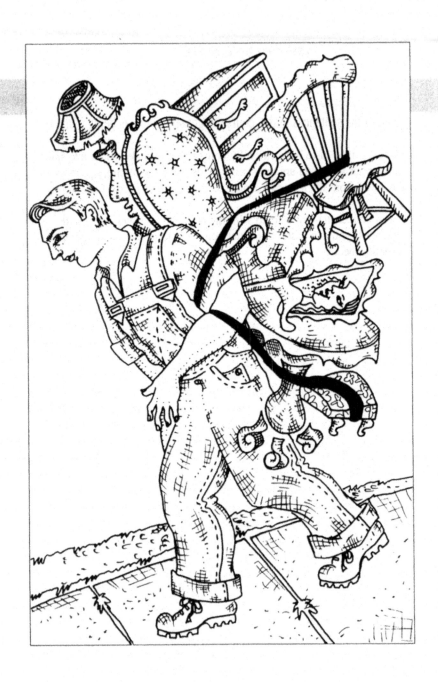

SECTION 2

HOME, FURNITURE, COLORS

FURNITURE

☐ **Think of each image in your mind's eye for about ten seconds**

- The Spanish for **bed** is **cama**.   (KAMA)
  Imagine a **camel** lying on your bed.

- The Spanish for **table** is **mesa**.   (MESA)
  Imagine a **messy** table.

- The Spanish for **chair** is **silla**.   (SEELYA)
  Imagine I **sell you** a large chair.

- The Spanish for **curtain** is **cortina**.   (KORTEENA)
  Imagine you fold your curtains into a
  concertina when you close them.

- The Spanish for **cupboard** is **armario**.   (ARMARYO)
  Imagine you keep an **armory** of weapons in
  your cupboard.

- The Spanish for **mirror** is **espejo**.   (ESPEHO)
  Imagine looking at **a speckled** mirror.

- The Spanish for **piano** is **piano**.   (PEE ANO)
  Imagine a bullfighter playing a **piano**.

- The Spanish for **clock** is **reloj**.   (RELO)
  Imagine **reloading** a clock.

- The Spanish for **shelf** is **estante**.   (ESTANTAY)
  Imagine putting up **instant** shelving.

- The Spanish for **drawer** is **cajón**.   (KAHON)
  Imagine a **car horn** sounds every time you open
  your drawer.

33

☐ *You can write your answers in*

- What is the English for **cajón**?   ————————

- What is the English for **estante**?   ————————

- What is the English for **reloj**?   ————————

- What is the English for **piano**?   ————————

- What is the English for **espejo**?   ————————

- What is the English for **armario**?   ————————

- What is the English for **cortina**?   ————————

- What is the English for **silla**?   ————————

- What is the English for **mesa**?   ————————

- What is the English for **cama**?   ————————

← *Look back for the answers*

34

□ *You can write your answers in*

- What is the Spanish for **drawer**? _____

- What is the Spanish for **shelf**? _____

- What is the Spanish for **clock**? _____

- What is the Spanish for **piano**? _____

- What is the Spanish for **mirror**? _____

- What is the Spanish for **cupboard**? _____

- What is the Spanish for **curtain**? _____

- What is the Spanish for **chair**? _____

- What is the Spanish for **table**? _____

- What is the Spanish for **bed**? _____

← *Look back for the answers*

SOME COLORS

☐ **Think of each image in your mind's eye for about ten seconds**

- The Spanish for **color** is **color.**   (KOLOR)
  Imagine a bullfighter with a coat of many
  colors.

- The Spanish for **black** is **negro.**   (NEGRO)
  Imagine watching your **knee grow** black and
  blue.

- The Spanish for **white** is **blanco.**   (BLANKO)
  Imagine a white piece of paper, completely
  blank.

- The Spanish for **gray** is **gris.**   (GREES)
  Imagine a patch of **grease** on the floor, all gray
  and horrible.

- The Spanish for **yellow** is **amarillo.**   (AMAREELYO)
  Imagine an **armadillo** painted all yellow.

- The Spanish for **red** is **rojo.**   (ROHO)
  Imagine seeing someone who is red and **raw.**

- The Spanish for **green** is **verde.**   (VERDAY)
  Imagine the composer **Verdi,** covered in green
  paint.

- The Spanish for **blue** is **azul.**   (ASUL)
  Imagine tipping a pot of blue paint over
  someone who is acting like **a fool.**

37

- What is the English for **azul**? _____

- What is the English for **verde**? _____

- What is the English for **rojo**? _____

- What is the English for **amarillo**? _____

- What is the English for **gris**? _____

- What is the English for **blanco**? _____

- What is the English for **negro**? _____

- What is the English for **color**? _____

← *Look back for the answers*

☐ *You can write your answers in*

- What is the Spanish for **blue**? _____

- What is the Spanish for **green**? _____

- What is the Spanish for **red**? _____

- What is the Spanish for **yellow**? _____

- What is the Spanish for **gray**? _____

- What is the Spanish for **white**? _____

- What is the Spanish for **black**? _____

- What is the Spanish for **color**? _____

← *Look back for the answers*

SOME MORE USEFUL ADJECTIVES

☐ **Think of each image in your mind's eye for about ten seconds**

- The Spanish for **pretty** is **bonito**.   (BONEETO)
  Imagine thinking "I have a pretty **bonny toe**."

- The Spanish for **free** is **libre**.   (LEEBRAY)
  Imagine giving someone **liberty** and setting the
  person free.

- The Spanish for **deep** is **profundo**.   (PROFOONDO)
  Imagine thinking deep, **profound** thoughts.

- The Spanish for **old** is **viejo**.   (VEE EHO)
  Imagine saying, "Good-bye, old man, **we hate
  you**."

- The Spanish for **little** is **pequeño**.   (PEKENYO)
  Imagine a little **bikini**.

☐ *You can write your answers in*

- What is the English for **viejo**? _____

- What is the English for **profundo**? _____

- What is the English for **libre**? _____

- What is the English for **bonito**? _____

- What is the English for **pequeño**? _____

← *Look back for the answers*

☐ *You can write your answers in*

- What is the Spanish for **old**? _____
- What is the Spanish for **deep**? _____
- What is the Spanish for **free**? _____
- What is the Spanish for **pretty**? _____
- What is the Spanish for **little**? _____

← *Look back for the answers*

ELEMENTARY GRAMMAR

You will remember from the last section that the ending of an adjective always agrees with the noun.

→ *For example:*

- *El toro está bonito* is *The bull is pretty*

- *La vaca está bonita* is *The cow is pretty*

You will probably have noticed, however, that you have been given some adjectives that do not end in *o* or *a*, like *libre* for *free*.

When this happens, you just leave the adjective alone, whatever it goes with.

→ *For example:*

- *The bull is free* is *El toro está libre*

- *The cow is free* is *La vaca está libre*

☐ **Now cover up the answers below and translate the following:**

☐ *(You can write your answers in)*

1. The quick jellyfish is quiet.

2. The quiet wasp is free.

3. The pretty chicken is fresh.

4. The quiet dog is fresh.

5. The black pig is free.

_____

_____

_____

_____

_____

_____

_____

☐ *The answers are:*

1. La medusa rápida está tranquila.

2. La avispa tranquila está libre.

3. El pollo bonito está fresco.

4. El perro tranquilo está fresco.

5. El puerco negro está libre.

☐ **Now cover up the answers below and translate the following:**

☐ *(You can write your answers in)*

1. El burro negro está libre.

2. El salmón bonito está fresco.

3. El pato verde está libre.

4. La rata blanca está rápida.

5. El toro negro está libre.

_____

_____

_____

_____

_____

_____

_____

_____

☐ *The answers are:*

1. The black donkey is free.

2. The pretty salmon is fresh.

3. The green duck is free.

4. The white rat is quick.

5. The black bull is free.

MORE FURNITURE

☐ **Think of each image in your mind's eye for about ten seconds**

- The Spanish for **stairs** (staircase) is **escalera**. (ESKALERA)
  Imagine **escalators** in your house instead of stairs.

- The Spanish for **floor** is **suelo**. (SOO ELO)
  Imagine a big **swelling** rising up in the floor.

- The Spanish for **wall** is (la) **pared**. (PARED)
  Imagine watching a **parade** from the top of a
  high wall.

- The Spanish for **kitchen** is **cocina**. (KOSEENA)
  Imagine being **cozy in** a kitchen.

- The Spanish for **bedroom** is **dormitorio**. (DORMEETORYO)
  Imagine your bedroom has been turned into a
  dormitory, with lots of people sleeping in it.

- The Spanish for **door** is **puerta**. (POO ERTA)
  Imagine a hotel **porter** opening a door for you.

- The Spanish for **window** is **ventana**. (VENTANA)
  Imagine a **vent on a** window.

- The Spanish for **garden** is **jardín**. (HARDEEN)
  Imagine someone working **hard in** the garden.

- The Spanish for **dining room** is **comedor**. (KOMEDOR)
  Imagine entertaining a **commodore** to dinner in
  your dining room.

- The Spanish for **cloakroom** is (el)
  guardarropa. (GOO ARDARROPA)
  Imagine someone paid to **guard a rope**
  in a cloakroom.
  (Note: **Guardarropa** is masculine even though
  it ends in *a*.)

☐ *You can write your answers in*

- What is the English for (el) **guardarropa**? ─────────

- What is the English for **comedor**? ─────────

- What is the English for **jardín**? ─────────

- What is the English for **ventana**? ─────────

- What is the English for **puerta**? ─────────

- What is the English for **dormitorio**? ─────────

- What is the English for **cocina**? ─────────

- What is the English for (la) **pared**? ─────────

- What is the English for **suelo**? ─────────

- What is the English for **escalera**? ─────────

← *Look back for the answers*

☐ *You can write your answers in*

- What is the Spanish for **cloakroom**? _____

- What is the Spanish for **dining room**? _____

- What is the Spanish for **garden**? _____

- What is the Spanish for **window**? _____

- What is the Spanish for **door**? _____

- What is the Spanish for **bedroom**? _____

- What is the Spanish for **kitchen**? _____

- What is the Spanish for **wall**? _____

- What is the Spanish for **floor**? _____

- What is the Spanish for **stairs**? _____

← *Look back for the answers*

SOME USEFUL VERBS

- The Spanish for **has** is **tiene.**   (TEE ENAY)
  Imagine someone *has* a **tinny** hat.

- The Spanish for **wants** is **quiere.**   (KEE ERAY)
  Imagine someone who *wants* to **query**
  everything.

- The Spanish for **eats** is **come.**   (KOMAY)
  Imagine telling someone to **come in** and *eat.*

☐ *You can write your answers in*

- What is the English for **come**?   _____

- What is the English for **quiere**?   _____

- What is the English for **tiene**?   _____

← *Look back for the answers*

☐ *You can write your answers in*

- What is the Spanish for **eats**?   _____

- What is the Spanish for **wants**?   _____

- What is the Spanish for **has**?   _____

← *Look back for the answers*

☐ **Now cover up the answers below and translate the following:**

☐ *(You can write your answers in)*

1. The duck has the goat.

2. The frog has the quiet cat.

3. The black bear wants the table.

4. The cow eats the quiet bird.

5. The dog eats the curtain.

_____

_____

_____

_____

_____

_____

_____

☐ *The answers are:*

1. El pato tiene la cabra.

2. La rana tiene el gato tranquilo.

3. El oso negro quiere la mesa.

4. La vaca come el pájaro tranquilo.

5. El perro come la cortina.

□ *(You can write your answers in)*

1. El burro quiere la cama vieja.

2. El mono quiere la cama profunda.

3. El oso tiene el piano gris.

4. La abeja come la cortina bonita.

5. La avispa quiere la silla dura.

_____

_____

_____

_____

_____

_____

_____

□ *The answers are:*

1. The donkey wants the old bed.

2. The monkey wants the deep bed.

3. The bear has the gray piano.

4. The bee eats the pretty curtain.

5. The wasp wants the hard chair.

SECTION 3

CLOTHES, FAMILY WORDS

CLOTHES

☐ **Think of each image in your mind's eye for about ten seconds**

* The Spanish for **hat** is **sombrero.**   (SOMBRERO)
  Imagine being given a large **sombrero** when
  you ask for a hat.

* The Spanish for **shoe** is **zapato.**   (SAPATO)
  Imagine a shoe on **the patio.**

* The Spanish for **trousers** (pants) is   (PANTALONES)
  pantalones.
  Imagine wearing baggy **pantaloons** for
  trousers.

* The Spanish for **skirt** is **falda.**   (FALDA)
  Imagine you **fold a** skirt away.

* The Spanish for **blouse** is **blusa.**   (BLOOSA)
  Imagine a **blue** blouse.

* The Spanish for **coat** is **abrigo.**   (ABREEGO)
  Imagine someone throwing **apricots** at your coat.

* The Spanish for **shirt** is **camisa.**   (KAMEESA)
  Imagine shouting, "**Come here, sir,** and get
  your shirt."

* The Spanish for **dress** is **vestido.**   (VESTEEDO)
  Imagine telling a little girl after putting her
  dress on that she should wear a **vest too!**

* The Spanish for **sandal** is **sandalia.**   (SANDALYA)
  Imagine a bullfighter in **sandals.**

* The Spanish for **bathing trunks** is **bañador.**   (BANYADOR)
  Imagine you **bang the door** with your bathing
  trunks.

57

☐ *You can write your answers in*

- What is the English for **bañador**? ————————

- What is the English for **sandalia**? ————————

- What is the English for **vestido**? ————————

- What is the English for **camisa**? ————————

- What is the English for **abrigo**? ————————

- What is the English for **blusa**? ————————

- What is the English for **falda**? ————————

- What is the English for **pantalones**? ————————

- What is the English for **zapato**? ————————

- What is the English for **sombrero**? ————————

← *Look back for the answers*

☐ *You can write your answers in*

- What is the Spanish for **bathing trunks**?   _____

- What is the Spanish for **sandal**?   _____

- What is the Spanish for **dress**?   _____

- What is the Spanish for **shirt**?   _____

- What is the Spanish for **coat**?   _____

- What is the Spanish for **blouse**?   _____

- What is the Spanish for **skirt**?   _____

- What is the Spanish for **trousers**?   _____

- What is the Spanish for **shoe**?   _____

- What is the Spanish for **hat**?   _____

← *Look back for the answers*

FAMILY

☐ **Think of each image in your mind's eye for about ten seconds**

* The Spanish for **father** is **padre.**   (PADRAY)
  Imagine your father dressed up as a **padre.**

* The Spanish for **mother** is **madre.**   (MADRAY)
  Imagine your mother very **mad** at you.

* The Spanish for **brother** is **hermano.**   (ERMANO)
  Imagine your brother is a very **hairy man, oh**
  dear.

* The Spanish for **sister** is **hermana.**   (ERMANA)
  Imagine your sister loves a **hairy man, ah** ha!

* The Spanish for **husband** is **marido.**   (MAREEDO)
  Imagine your husband is **married!**

* The Spanish for **wife** is **mujer.**   (MOOHER)
  Imagine a wife dressed in a **mohair** coat.

* The Spanish for **boy** is **muchacho.**   (MOOCHACHO)
  Imagine a boy who **moos** while putting on a
  cha-**cha show: MOO-CHA-CHO.**

* The Spanish for **girl** is **muchacha.**   (MOOCHACHA)
  Imagine a girl who **moos,** then does a **cha-cha:**
  MOO-CHA-CHA.

* The Spanish for **son** is **hijo.**   (EEHO)
  Imagine your son going **EE-HO,** just like a
  donkey.

* The Spanish for **daughter** is **hija.**   (EEHA)
  Imagine your daughter sounding like a female
  donkey, with an *a* at the end: **EE-HA.**

You can write your answers in

- What is the English for **hija**? _____

- What is the English for **hijo**? _____

- What is the English for **muchacha**? _____

- What is the English for **muchacho**? _____

- What is the English for **mujer**? _____

- What is the English for **marido**? _____

- What is the English for **hermana**? _____

- What is the English for **hermano**? _____

- What is the English for **madre**? _____

- What is the English for **padre**? _____

← *Look back for the answers*

☐ *You can write your answers in*

- What is the Spanish for **daughter**? _____

- What is the Spanish for **son**? _____

- What is the Spanish for **girl**? _____

- What is the Spanish for **boy**? _____

- What is the Spanish for **wife**? _____

- What is the Spanish for **husband**? _____

- What is the Spanish for **sister**? _____

- What is the Spanish for **brother**? _____

- What is the Spanish for **mother**? _____

- What is the Spanish for **father**? _____

← *Look back for the answers*

A FEW USEFUL WORDS

☐ **Think of each image in your mind's eye for about ten seconds**

- The Spanish for **only** is **solamente.**   (SOLAMENTAY)
  Imagine thinking, "If *only* **Solomon meant it.**"

- The Spanish for **very** is **muy.**   (MOO EE)
  Imagine **mwe** are *very* good at Spanish.

- The Spanish for **yes** is **sí.**   (SEE)
  Imagine answering, "*Yes.* **Sí,** Señor! Yes, sir."

- The Spanish for **no** is **no.**   (NO)
  Imagine thinking, "**No! No!** Mr. Bullfighter."

- The Spanish for **not** is **no.**   (NO)
  Imagine saying, "No, *not*, **no!**"

65

☐ *You can write your answers in*

- What is the English for **no**? _____

- What is the English for **sí**? _____

- What is the English for **muy**? _____

- What is the English for **solamente**? _____

← *Look back for the answers*

66

□ *You can write your answers in*

- What is the Spanish for **no** or **not**? _____

- What is the Spanish for **yes**? _____

- What is the Spanish for **very**? _____

- What is the Spanish for **only**? _____

← *Look back for the answers*

ELEMENTARY GRAMMAR

In this section, you will be shown how to use the words *and*, *but*, and *or*.

☐ The Spanish for *and* is y (pronounced EE).

➜ *So,*

- *pretty and bad* is *bonito y malo*

☐ The Spanish for *but* is *pero*.

This sounds like *perro*, but the sound of the *r* is shorter.

➜ *So,*

- *pretty but bad* is *bonito pero malo*

☐ The Spanish for *or* is *o*.

O is the first letter of the word *or*. It is as if the Spaniards have forgotten to put the *r* on the word.

➜ *So,*

- *pretty or bad* is *bonito o malo*

☐ **Now cover up the answers below and translate the following:**

☐ *(You can write your answers in)*

1. The dog has the hat and the skirt.

2. The frog wants the skirt and the dress.

3. The fly has the bathing trunks and the shirt.

4. The father eats the mother but not the son.

5. The boy wants the pretty goat.

_____

_____

_____

_____

_____

_____

_____

_____

☐ *The answers are:*

1. El perro tiene el sombrero y la falda.

2. La rana quiere la falda y el vestido.

3. La mosca tiene el bañador y la camisa.

4. El padre come a la madre pero no al hijo.

5. El muchacho quiere la cabra bonita.

☐ *(You can write your answers in)*

1. El marido quiere el reloj viejo pero no el piano.

2. El gato pequeño quiere el cajón o el armario.

3. La muchacha bonita tiene el estante gris.

4. La mosca azul come la puerta amarilla.

5. El hermano quiere el guardarropa y la hermana quiere el dormitorio.

_____

_____

_____

_____

_____

_____

☐ *The answers are:*

1. The husband wants the old clock but not the piano.

2. The little cat wants the drawer or the cupboard.

3. The pretty girl has the gray shelf.

4. The blue fly eats the yellow door.

5. The brother wants the cloakroom and the sister wants the bedroom.

SOME MORE ELEMENTARY GRAMMAR

The next grammar point is about the word *a*.

The Spanish for this word as used in *a pig* or *a cat* or *an animal* is *un* (pronounced OON).

→ *For example:*

- *a pig*   is *un puerco*

- *a dog*   is *un perro*

- *a cat*   is *un gato*

- *an animal* is *un animal*

When the word is feminine, then you add the feminine ending *a* to the word *un* to make *una* (pronounced OONA).

→ *For example:*

- *a cow*   is *una vaca*

- *a goat*   is *una cabra*

- *a table*   is *una mesa*

☐ *(You can write your answers in)*

1. A red cow eats a window.

2. A wife wants a dining room and a kitchen.

3. A bad pig wants a shoe.

4. A boy has a fresh shirt and a red coat.

5. A quick girl wants a quiet bed.

_____

_____

_____

_____

_____

_____

_____

☐ *The answers are:*

1. Una vaca roja come una ventana.

2. Una mujer quiere un comedor y una cocina.

3. Un puerco malo quiere un zapato.

4. Un muchacho tiene una camisa fresca y un abrigo rojo.

5. Una muchacha rápida quiere una cama tranquila.

☐ **Now cover up the answers below and translate the following:**

☐ *(You can write your answers in)*

1. Un animal tiene un armario duro.

2. El puerco quiere un guardarropa.

3. El pájaro bonito tiene un jardín verde.

4. El pato quiere el comedor.

5. Un pollo tiene un estante verde.

_____

_____

_____

_____

_____

_____

_____

☐ *The answers are:*

1. An animal has a hard cupboard.

2. The pig wants a cloakroom.

3. The pretty bird has a green garden.

4. The duck wants the dining room.

5. A chicken has a green shelf.

73

A NUMBER OF USEFUL WORDS

☐ **Think of each image in your mind's eye for about ten seconds**

- The Spanish for **friend** is **amigo.** (AMEEGO)
  Imagine telling my friend that **I may go** if the
  friend is not more pleasant to me.

- The Spanish for **afternoon** is (la) **tarde.** (TARDAY)
  Imagine being so late and **tardy** at getting up
  that it is the afternoon before you appear.

- The Spanish for **storm** is **tormenta.** (TORMENTA)
  Imagine being **tormented** by a storm.

- The Spanish for **receptionist** (RESEPSEEONEESTA)
  is **recepcionista.**
  Imagine a bullfighter asking a **receptionist**
  for a room.

- The Spanish for **number** is **número.** (NOOMERO)
  Imagine someone giving you **numerous**
  numbers for a telephone number.

- The Spanish for **paper** is **papel.** (PAPEL)
  Imagine everyone throwing paper during a
  papal visit.

- The Spanish for **room** is (la) **habitación.** (ABEETASYON)
  Imagine thinking, "This room is not fit for
  human **habitation.**"

- The Spanish for **mail box** is **buzón.** (BOOSON)
  Imagine a **bus on** top of a mail box.

- The Spanish for **bath** is **baño.** (BANYO)
  Imagine they **ban you** from having a bath.

- The Spanish for **morning** is **mañana.** (MANYANA)
  Imagine meeting a **man you know** every
  morning.

75

□ *You can write your answers in*

- What is the English for **mañana**? ———————————

- What is the English for **baño**? ———————————

- What is the English for **buzón**? ———————————

- What is the English for (la) **habitación**? ———————————

- What is the English for **papel**? ———————————

- What is the English for **número**? ———————————

- What is the English for **recepcionista**? ———————————

- What is the English for **tormenta**? ———————————

- What is the English for (la) **tarde**? ———————————

- What is the English for **amigo**? ———————————

← *Look back for the answers*

☐ *You can write your answers in*

- What is the Spanish for **morning**?   _____

- What is the Spanish for **bath**?   _____

- What is the Spanish for **mail box**?   _____

- What is the Spanish for **room**?   _____

- What is the Spanish for **paper**?   _____

- What is the Spanish for **number**?   _____

- What is the Spanish for **receptionist**?   _____

- What is the Spanish for **storm**?   _____

- What is the Spanish for **afternoon**?   _____

- What is the Spanish for **friend**?   _____

← *Look back for the answers*

☐ *(You can write your answers in)*

1. A friend eats a receptionist.

2. A dog wants a red bath and a red mail box.

3. A black cat wants the white paper and a quiet room.

4. The dog wants the black paper and the cat has a number.

5. The morning is fresh and the afternoon is fresh.

_____

_____

_____

_____

_____

_____

_____

_____

☐ *The answers are:*

1. Un amigo come a una recepcionista.

2. Un perro quiere un baño rojo y un buzón rojo.

3. Un gato negro quiere el papel blanco y una habitación tranquila.

4. El perro quiere el papel negro y el gato tiene un número.

5. La mañana está fresca y la tarde está fresca.

☐ Now cover up the answers below and translate the following:

☐ *(You can write your answers in)*

1. El perro quiere un buzón.

2. La tormenta está tranquila.

3. La recepcionista quiere un número.

4. La mañana está tranquila y la tarde está tranquila.

5. El amigo está rápido.

_____

_____

_____

_____

_____

_____

_____

☐ *The answers are:*

1. The dog wants a mail box.

2. The storm is quiet.

3. The receptionist wants a number.

4. The morning is quiet and the afternoon is quiet.

5. The friend is quick.

SECTION 4

IN THE COUNTRY

☐ **Think of each image in your mind's eye for about ten seconds**

- The Spanish for **flower** is (la) **flor.**   (FLOR)
  Imagine flowers scattered all over the **floor.**

- The Spanish for **tree** is **árbol.**   (ARBOL)
  Imagine throwing a **hard ball** against a tree.

- The Spanish for **plant** is **planta.**   (PLANTA)
  Imagine giving a bullfighter a potted **plant.**

- The Spanish for **fruit** is **fruta.**   (FROOTA)
  Imagine throwing **fruit** at a bullfighter.

- The Spanish for **path** is **senda.**   (SENDA)
  Imagine you **send a** friend along a path.

☐ *You can write your answers in*

- What is the English for **senda**?　　　　_____

- What is the English for **fruta**?　　　　_____

- What is the English for **planta**?　　　　_____

- What is the English for **árbol**?　　　　_____

- What is the English for (la) **flor**?　　　　_____

← *Look back for the answers*

☐ *You can write your answers in*

- What is the Spanish for **path**? _____
- What is the Spanish for **fruit**? _____
- What is the Spanish for **plant**? _____
- What is the Spanish for **tree**? _____
- What is the Spanish for **flower**? _____

← *Look back for the answers*

TIME

☐ **Think of each image in your mind's eye for about ten seconds**

- The Spanish for **time** is **tiempo.**   (TEE EMPO)
  Imagine keeping time to the **tempo** of the
  music.

- The Spanish for **second** is **segundo.**   (SEGOONDO)
  Imagine a bullfighter tapping his feet every
  second.

- The Spanish for **minute** is **minuto.**   (MEENOOTO)
  Imagine a bullfighter killing a bull once a
  minute.

- The Spanish for **hour** is **hora.**   (ORA)
  Imagine waiting in **horror** for the hour to
  strike.

- The Spanish for **week** is **semana.**   (SEMANA)
  Imagine going to a **seminar** once a week.

- The Spanish for **month** is **mes.**   (MES)
  Imagine being in a **mess** once a month.

- The Spanish for **year** is **año.**   (ANYO)
  Imagine a year is **annual.**

- The Spanish for **day** is (el) **día.**   (DEE A)
  Imagine thinking everything is **dear** during the
  day.
  (Note: This is masculine even though it ends in *a*.)

- The Spanish for **night** is (la) **noche.**   (NOCHAY)
  Imagine **nocturnal** animals are out at night.

- The Spanish for **yesterday** is **ayer.**   (A YER)
  Imagine thinking that prices were **higher**
  yesterday.

☐ *You can write your answers in*

- What is the English for **ayer**? _____

- What is the English for (la) **noche**? _____

- What is the English for (el) **día**? _____

- What is the English for **año**? _____

- What is the English for **mes**? _____

- What is the English for **semana**? _____

- What is the English for **hora**? _____

- What is the English for **minuto**? _____

- What is the English for **segundo**? _____

- What is the English for **tiempo**? _____

← *Look back for the answers*

☐ *You can write your answers in*

- What is the Spanish for **yesterday**? _____

- What is the Spanish for **night**? _____

- What is the Spanish for **day**? _____

- What is the Spanish for **year**? _____

- What is the Spanish for **month**? _____

- What is the Spanish for **week**? _____

- What is the Spanish for **hour**? _____

- What is the Spanish for **minute**? _____

- What is the Spanish for **second**? _____

- What is the Spanish for **time**? _____

← *Look back for the answers*

SOME MORE USEFUL WORDS

☐ **Think of each image in your mind's eye for about ten seconds**

- The Spanish for **soon** is **pronto.**   (PRONTO)
  Imagine telling someone that she had better do
  something *soon,* **pronto.**

- The Spanish for **much** is **mucho.**   (MOOCHO)
  Imagine someone who **mooches** from you *much*
  of the time.
  (**Mucho** and **much** also sound similar.)

- The Spanish for **more** is **más.**   (MAS)
  Imagine being given a **mass** of food, and your
  host giving you *more* and more.

- The Spanish for **less** is **menos.**   (MENOS)
  Imagine getting *less*—a **minus** quantity.

- The Spanish for **always** is **siempre.**   (SEE EMPRAY)
  Imagine someone who *always* **simpers.**

☐ *You can write your answers in*

- What is the English for **siempre**?   _____

- What is the English for **menos**?   _____

- What is the English for **más**?   _____

- What is the English for **mucho**?   _____

- What is the English for **pronto**?   _____

← *Look back for the answers*

90

☐ *You can write your answers in*

- What is the Spanish for **always**? _____

- What is the Spanish for **less**? _____

- What is the Spanish for **more**? _____

- What is the Spanish for **much**? _____

- What is the Spanish for **soon**? _____

← *Look back for the answers*

ELEMENTARY GRAMMAR

In the first section, we learned that the Spanish for *is* is *está*.

➡ *For example:*

* *La vaca está fresca* is *The cow is fresh*

There are, however, two words for the word *is* in Spanish—*está* and *es*. (*Es* is pronounced like the letter *s*.)

You use *está* for something temporary, and *es* for something permanent.

➡ *For example:*

If you mean by *The dog is quick* that it is a quick dog, it always moves quickly, then the Spanish is:

* *El perro es rápido*. (It is a quick dog.)

If, on the other hand, you mean that the dog was quick just now, when it ran away, then the Spanish is:

* *El perro está rápido*.

➡ *Here is another example:*

* *The cat is good.*

In Spanish, *el gato es bueno* means it is a good cat.

El gato está bueno means that it is being good at the minute.

If you use the word *today*, this will almost always mean that the description will be temporary and you would use the word *está*.

* The Spanish word for *today* is *hoy*.

  Imagine thinking "*Oy!* Today's the day."

So, the sentence *The cat is good today* is *El gato está bueno hoy*.

☐ **Now cover up the answers below and translate the following:**

☐ *(You can write your answers in)*

1. La sandalia es negra.

2. El árbol es muy pequeño.

3. El pez está fresco.

4. La senda es verde y la planta es blanca.

5. La cama es solamente dura.

_____

_____

_____

_____

_____

_____

_____

☐ *The answers are:*

1. The sandal is black.

2. The tree is very small.

3. The fish is fresh.

4. The path is green and the plant is white.

5. The bed is only hard.

93

☐ **Now cover up the answers below and translate the following:**

☐ *(You can write your answers in)*

1. The cow is quick. *(It is a quick cow.)*

2. The mouse is quick. *(The mouse moved quickly.)*

3. The donkey is quiet. *(The donkey is quiet at the minute.)*

4. The fish is quiet. *(It is a quiet fish.)*

5. The fly is fresh. *(The fly is fresh now.)*

_____

_____

_____

_____

_____

_____

☐ *The answers are:*

1. La vaca es rápida.

2. El ratón está rápido.

3. El burro está tranquilo.

4. El pez es tranquilo.

5. La mosca está fresca.

You must not worry if you do not get everything right at this stage. This is about the hardest part of the grammar.

All you need to remember is why *es* and *está* are different.

ELEMENTARY GRAMMAR

The Spanish for *are* is *son*, if *are* is meant in the permanent sense.

➜ *So,*

- *The dog and the cat are quiet* is *El perro y el gato son tranquilos.*

If *are* is used in a temporary sense, then the Spanish word for it is *están.*

➜ *So,*

- *The dog and the cat are quiet today* is *El perro y el gato están tranquilos hoy.*

Please note that you have to make the adjective plural too, so you add an *s* to change *tranquilo* into *tranquilos.*

You should also note:

When you have a masculine and feminine word together, like *The dog and the frog are black*, then the end of the adjective (*negro*) is always *masculine* and plural.

➜ *So,*

- *The dog and the frog are black* is *El perro y la rana son negros.*

☐ *(You can write your answers in)*

1. The bed and the table are always black.

2. The blue curtain and the green drawer are old.

3. The garden and the coat are fresh and green.

4. The cow and the bull are very good.

5. The shirt and the coat are always black.

_____

_____

_____

_____

_____

_____

_____

☐ *The answers are:*

1. La cama y la mesa son siempre negras.

2. La cortina azul y el cajón verde son viejos.

3. El jardín y el abrigo son frescos y verdes.

4. La vaca y el toro son (or están) muy buenos.

5. La camisa y el abrigo son siempre negros.

Now cover up the answers below and translate the following:

☐ *(You can write your answers in)*

1. El suelo y la pared son solamente amarillos.

2. La flor y el árbol están muy bonitos hoy.

3. El baño es muy profundo.

4. La planta y la camisa son rojas.

5. El oso está malo.

_____

_____

_____

_____

_____

_____

_____

☐ *The answers are:*

1. The floor and the wall are only yellow.

2. The flower and the tree are very pretty today.

3. The bath is very deep.

4. The plant and the shirt are red.

5. The bear is bad.

THE DAYS OF THE WEEK

☐ **Think of each image in your mind's eye for about ten seconds**

- The Spanish for **Monday** is **lunes.**   (LOONAYS)
  Imagine only **loonies** go to work on Monday.

- The Spanish for **Tuesday** is **martes.**   (MARTAYS)
  Imagine you always burn **martyrs** on Tuesdays.

- The Spanish for **Wednesday** is **miércoles.**   (MEE ERCOLAYS)
  Imagine praying for **miracles** on Wednesday
  so that the end of the week will come quickly.

- The Spanish for **Thursday** is **jueves.**   (HOO EVAYS)
  Imagine you **wave us** good-bye on Thursdays.

- The Spanish for **Friday** is **viernes.**   (VEE ERNAYS)
  Imagine showing your **bare knees** on Friday,
  to celebrate the end of the week.

- The Spanish for **Saturday** is **sábado.**   (SABADO)
  Imagine Saturday is the Jewish **sabbath.**

- The Spanish for **Sunday** is **domingo.**   (DOMEENGO)
  Imagine you play **dominoes** with your family
  on Sunday evening before shoving them off
  to bed.

□ *You can write your answers in*

- What is the English for **domingo**? _____
- What is the English for **sábado**? _____
- What is the English for **viernes**? _____
- What is the English for **jueves**? _____
- What is the English for **miércoles**? _____
- What is the English for **martes**? _____
- What is the English for **lunes**? _____

← *Look back for the answers*

100

☐ *You can write your answers in*

- What is the Spanish for **Sunday**?   _____

- What is the Spanish for **Saturday**?   _____

- What is the Spanish for **Friday**?   _____

- What is the Spanish for **Thursday**?   _____

- What is the Spanish for **Wednesday**?   _____

- What is the Spanish for **Tuesday**?   _____

- What is the Spanish for **Monday**?   _____

← *Look back for the answers*

PLEASE NOTE:

You do not say the word *on* when talking about the days of the week; you leave out the word *on* and use *el*.

➜ *So,*

- *on Tuesday* is *el martes,* if you mean *next Tuesday.*

If you mean *every Tuesday* (as you would if you said *on Tuesdays*), then in Spanish you make it plural and use *los*.

➜ *So,*

- *on Tuesdays* is *los martes*

- *on Sundays* is *los domingos*

and so on.

- *The dog eats on Tuesdays* is *El perro come los martes.*

- *The cow eats on Saturdays* is *La vaca come los sábados.*

☐ **Now cover up the answers below and translate the following:**

☐ *(You can write your answers in)*

1. Los martes el perro come la fruta.

2. El perro come los lunes, los viernes, los sábados y los domingos.

3. No, el gato no come los jueves y los miércoles.

4. Los domingos las noches están negras.

5. El burro quiere menos pato y más pollo.

_____

_____

_____

_____

_____

_____

_____

☐ *The answers are:*

1. On Tuesdays the dog eats the fruit.

2. The dog eats on Mondays, Fridays, Saturdays, and Sundays.

3. No, the cat does not eat on Thursdays and Wednesdays.

4. On Sundays the nights are black.

5. The donkey wants less duck and more chicken.

ELEMENTARY GRAMMAR

The way to ask questions in Spanish when you are speaking is by tone of voice; you do not need to change the word order.

- *¿Es un toro?* is *Is it a bull?*

In Spanish, you leave out words like *he, I, you, it* and so on.

→ *So,*

- *It is a bull*   is *Es un toro*

- *He has a bull*   is *Tiene un toro*

- *Does he have a bull?* is *¿Tiene un toro?*

Note the use of the upside-down question mark in written Spanish, which indicates that a question is coming up.

☐ **Now cover up the answers below and translate the following:**

☐ *(You can write your answers in)*

1. Is it a pig?

2. He has a dog.

3. Is it a table?

4. Does he have a flower?

5. He eats a goat.

_____

_____

_____

_____

_____

_____

_____

_____

☐ *The answers are:*

1. ¿Es un puerco?

2. Tiene un perro.

3. ¿Es una mesa?

4. ¿Tiene una flor?

5. Come una cabra.

□ **Now cover up the answers below and translate the following:**

□ *(You can write your answers in)*

1. Es la semana, la hora y el día.

2. ¿Es un árbol verde?

3. ¿Es la noche?

4. ¿Es la senda o la escalera?

5. Es la hija, no el hijo.

_____

_____

_____

_____

_____

_____

_____

□ *The answers are:*

1. It is the week, the hour, and the day.

2. Is it a green tree?

3. Is it the night?

4. Is it the path or the stairs?

5. It is the daughter, not the son.

SECTION 5

IN A RESTAURANT, NUMBERS, TELLING TIME

IN A RESTAURANT

☐ **Think of each image in your mind's eye for about ten seconds**

- The Spanish for **restaurant** is **restaurante.** (RESTA OORANTAY)
  Imagine a bullfighter in your **restaurant.**

- The Spanish for **waitress** is **camarera.** (KAMARERA)
  Imagine a waitress with a **camera** slung around her neck.

- The Spanish for **cup** is **taza.** (TASA)
  Imagine a cup with a **tassel** dangling from the handle.

- The Spanish for **bill** is **cuenta.** (KOO ENTA)
  Imagine your friend **went a**way when it came to paying the bill.

- The Spanish for **menu** is **menú.** (MENOO)
  Imagine a bullfighter studying the **menu.**

- The Spanish for **plate** is **plato.** (PLATO)
  Imagine you climb a mountain and reach a **plateau** all covered with white plates.

- The Spanish for **knife** is **cuchillo.** (KOOCHEELYO)
  Imagine someone with a knife saying, "With this I **could chill you.**"

- The Spanish for **fork** is **tenedor.** (TENEDOR)
  Imagine prodding a piece of meat with a fork to make sure it is **tender.**

- The Spanish for **tablecloth** is **mantel.** (MANTEL)
  Imagine a tablecloth on the **mantel**piece.

- The Spanish for **bottle** is **botella.** (BOTELYA)
  Imagine throwing a **bottle** at a bullfighter.

107

☐ *You can write your answers in*

- What is the English for **botella**? _____

- What is the English for **mantel**? _____

- What is the English for **tenedor**? _____

- What is the English for **cuchillo**? _____

- What is the English for **plato**? _____

- What is the English for **menú**? _____

- What is the English for **cuenta**? _____

- What is the English for **taza**? _____

- What is the English for **camarera**? _____

- What is the English for **restaurante**? _____

← *Look back for the answers*

☐ *You can write your answers in*

- What is the Spanish for **bottle**? _____

- What is the Spanish for **tablecloth**? _____

- What is the Spanish for **fork**? _____

- What is the Spanish for **knife**? _____

- What is the Spanish for **plate**? _____

- What is the Spanish for **menu**? _____

- What is the Spanish for **bill**? _____

- What is the Spanish for **cup**? _____

- What is the Spanish for **waitress**? _____

- What is the Spanish for **restaurant**? _____

← *Look back for the answers*

NUMBERS

☐ **Think of each image in your mind's eye for about ten seconds**

- The Spanish for **one** is **uno.** (OONO)
  Imagine **you know** one.

- The Spanish for **two** is **dos.** (DOS)
  Imagine you **toss** two coins in the air.

- The Spanish for **three** is **tres.** (TRES)
  Imagine three **trees** in front of you.

- The Spanish for **four** is **cuatro.** (KOO ATRO)
  Imagine drinking four bottles of **cointreau.**

- The Spanish for **five** is **cinco.** (SEENKO)
  Imagine being bathed in the **sink o** when you
  were five years old.

- The Spanish for **six** is **seis.** (SE EES)
  Imagine some who **says** six.

- The Spanish for **seven** is **siete.** (SEE ETAY)
  Imagine your **settee** has seven large spots on it.

- The Spanish for **eight** is **ocho.** (OCHO)
  Imagine the number eight painted in **ochre.**

- The Spanish for **nine** is **nueve.** (NOO EVAY)
  Imagine dialing 911 for the **navy.**

- The Spanish for **zero** is **cero.** (SERO)
  Imagine **zero** is nothing to a bullfighter.

☐ *You can write your answers in*

- What is the English for **uno**? _____

- What is the English for **dos**? _____

- What is the English for **tres**? _____

- What is the English for **cuatro**? _____

- What is the English for **cinco**? _____

- What is the English for **seis**? _____

- What is the English for **siete**? _____

- What is the English for **ocho**? _____

- What is the English for **nueve**? _____

- What is the English for **cero**? _____

← *Look back for the answers*

☐ *You can write your answers in*

- What is the Spanish for **one**? _____

- What is the Spanish for **two**? _____

- What is the Spanish for **three**? _____

- What is the Spanish for **four**? _____

- What is the Spanish for **five**? _____

- What is the Spanish for **six**? _____

- What is the Spanish for **seven**? _____

- What is the Spanish for **eight**? _____

- What is the Spanish for **nine**? _____

- What is the Spanish for **zero**? _____

← *Look back for the answers*

ELEMENTARY GRAMMAR: Plurals

The plurals in Spanish are very simple.

☐ For *masculine* plurals, *el* becomes *los* and the noun adds an *s*.

➜ *For example:*

- *el plato*   becomes *los platos* (the plates)
- *el cuchillo*   becomes *los cuchillos*
- *el sombrero* becomes *los sombreros*

☐ For *feminine* words, the *la* becomes *las* and the noun also adds an *s*.

➜ *For example:*

- *la cabra* becomes *las cabras* (the goats)
- *la mesa*   becomes *las mesas*
- *la blusa* becomes *las blusas*

If a word does not end in a vowel, then you simply add *es*.

➜ *For example:*

- *el tenedor* becomes *los tenedores* (the forks)
- *el mantel*   becomes *los manteles*

☐ As we have already seen with *tranquilos*, adjectives also add an *s* when they are plural.

➜ *So,*

- *the free pigs*   is *los puercos libres*
- *the quiet mice* is *los ratones tranquilos*
- *the red tables* is *las mesas rojas*

Numbers do not take a plural ending.

☐ **Now cover up the answers below and translate the following:**

☐ *(You can write your answers in)*

1. Three cups are old.

2. Five plates are very good.

3. The knives and the forks are very hard.

4. The tablecloths and the bottles are always green.

5. Two menus are very bad.

_____

_____

_____

_____

_____

_____

_____

☐ *The answers are:*

1. Tres tazas son viejas.

2. Cinco platos son muy buenos.

3. Los cuchillos y los tenedores son muy duros.

4. Los manteles y las botellas son siempre verdes.

5. Dos menús son muy malos.

115

☐ Now cover up the answers below and translate the following:

☐ *(You can write your answers in)*

1. Siete días son una semana.

2. Los restaurantes son siempre buenos.

3. Las cuentas son muy buenas.

4. Los días son buenos, y las noches son buenas.

5. Los pantalones son muy negros.

_____

_____

_____

_____

_____

_____

_____

_____

☐ *The answers are:*

1. Seven days are a week.

2. The restaurants are always good.

3. The bills are very good.

4. The days are good, and the nights are good.

5. The trousers (pants) are very black.

SOME MORE USEFUL WORDS

☐ **Think of each image in your mind's eye for about ten seconds**

- The Spanish for **on** is **en**.   (EN)
  Imagine a big letter **n** written *on* a table.

- The Spanish for **in** is also **en**.   (EN)
  Imagine looking *in* a box and seeing a large
  letter **n**.

- The Spanish for **under** is **debajo de**.   (DEBAHO DAY)
  Imagine seeing a **debacle** *under* the table.

- The Spanish for **outside** is **fuera de**.   (FOO ERA DAY)
  Imagine you are *outside* **for a day**.

☐ *You can write your answers in*

- What is the English for **en**? _____

- What is the English for **debajo de**? _____

- What is the English for **fuera de**? _____

← *Look back for the answers*

118

☐ *You can write your answers in*

- What is the Spanish for **in**? _____

- What is the Spanish for **on**? _____

- What is the Spanish for **under**? _____

- What is the Spanish for **outside**? _____

← *Look back for the answers*

119

Please note that place words (prepositions) in Spanish are tricky and you will sometimes make mistakes. Do not worry though, as you will be understood.

There is one important point to remember:

When you use place words like *in, on, under,* etc., then the word for *is* is always *está,* even if the thing is always in a particular place.

☐ **Now cover up the answers below and translate the following:**

☐ *(You can write your answers in)*

1. The cup is on the table.

2. The plate is in the cupboard.

3. The knife is under a table.

4. The fruit is on the plate.

5. A waitress is outside a restaurant.

_____

_____

_____

_____

_____

_____

_____

☐ *The answers are:*

1. La taza está en la mesa.

2. El plato está en el armario.

3. El cuchillo está debajo de una mesa.

4. La fruta está en el plato.

5. Una camarera está fuera de un restaurante.

☐ **Now cover up the answers below and translate the following:**

☐ *(You can write your answers in)*

1. Seis camareras están debajo de la mesa.

2. Cuatro tenedores están en el cajón.

3. El marido y la mujer están en un restaurante.

4. El pez está fuera de un guardarropa.

5. El perro está en el armario amarillo.

_____

_____

_____

_____

_____

_____

☐ *The answers are:*

1. Six waitresses are under the table.

2. Four forks are in the drawer.

3. The husband and the wife are in a restaurant.

4. The fish is outside a cloakroom.

5. The dog is on (or in) the yellow cupboard.

NUMBERS

☐ **Think of each image in your mind's eye for about ten seconds**

- The Spanish for **ten** is **diez**.   (DEE ES)
  Imagine putting someone to **death** at ten
  o'clock.

- The Spanish for **eleven** is **once**.   (ONSAY)
  Imagine eleven football players **on the** field.

- The Spanish for **twelve** is **doce**.   (DOSAY)
  Imagine a dozen **dozy** people.

- The Spanish for **twenty** is **veinte**.   (VE EENTAY)
  Imagine a German saying, "Your vision is
  tventy-tventy."

- The Spanish for **twenty-five** is   (VE EENTEESEENKO)
  veinticinco.
  Imagine at the age of 25 you **invented sinks**.

- The Spanish for **quarter** is **cuarto**.   (KOO ARTO)
  Imagine asking a bullfighter for a **quarter** of
  beef.

- The Spanish for **half** is **media**.   (MEDYA)
  Imagine someone **made you** cut yourself in
  half.

123

☐ *You can write your answers in*

- What is the English for **diez**?   _____

- What is the English for **once**?   _____

- What is the English for **doce**?   _____

- What is the English for **veinte**?   _____

- What is the English for **veinticinco**?   _____

- What is the English for **cuarto**?   _____

- What is the English for **media**?   _____

← *Look back for the answers*

☐ *You can write your answers in*

- What is the Spanish for **ten**?   _____

- What is the Spanish for **eleven**?   _____

- What is the Spanish for **twelve**?   _____

- What is the Spanish for **twenty**?   _____

- What is the Spanish for **twenty-five**?   _____

- What is the Spanish for **quarter**?   _____

- What is the Spanish for **half**?   _____

← *Look back for the answers*

TELLING TIME

As you learned earlier, the Spanish for *the hour* is *la hora,* which is, of course, *feminine.*

The Spanish for *what* is *qué* (pronounced KAY) so:

- *What time is it?* is *¿Qué hora es?*—literally, *What hour is?*

To answer this question by saying, for example, *It is one o'clock,* you say something in Spanish that translates literally as *(It) is the one: Es la una.*

The word *hour* is not said, but is understood.

Note that the word *the* is feminine because the word *hour* is feminine.

- *It is two o'clock* becomes *(They) are the two* or *Son las dos*

Here *las* is used because *horas* is plural.

➡ *Similarly,*

- *It is three o'clock* is *Son las tres*

- *It is eleven o'clock* is *Son las once*

☐ Now cover up the answers below and translate the following:

☐ *(You can write your answers in)*

1. It is five o'clock.

2. It is seven o'clock.

3. It is nine o'clock.

4. It is ten o'clock.

5. It is two o'clock.

_____

_____

_____

_____

_____

_____

_____

☐ *The answers are:*

1. Son las cinco.

2. Son las siete.

3. Son las nueve.

4. Son las diez.

5. Son las dos.

TELLING TIME: PARTS OF AN HOUR

When you want to say *It is quarter after* or *half past* or *five after* the hour you say, for example:

- *They are seven and half* or *Son las siete y media*

To say *It is five after three*, you say *Son las tres y cinco*

To say *It is twenty after eight*, you say *Son las ocho y veinte*

When you want to say *It is quarter to the hour* or *twenty to the hour* or *five to the hour* or *twenty to eight*, etc., in Spanish you do as follows:

- *They are eight minus twenty* is *Son las ocho menos veinte*

- *It is quarter to five* is *Son las cinco menos cuarto*

- *It is five to two* is *Son las dos menos cinco*

The only exception to this is with the hour *one*, which is singular.

➔ *So,*

- *It is quarter to one* is *Es la una menos cuarto*

☐ **Now cover up the answers below and translate the following:**

☐ *(You can write your answers in)*

1. It is half past three.

2. It is four o'clock.

3. It is quarter to six.

4. It is ten to seven.

5. It is half past nine.

6. It is ten to one.

7. It is three o'clock.

_____

_____

_____

_____

_____

☐ *The answers are:*

1. Son las tres y media.

2. Son las cuatro.

3. Son las seis menos cuarto.

4. Son las siete menos diez.

5. Son las nueve y media.

6. Es la una menos diez.

7. Son las tres.

129

SECTION 6

☐ **Think of each image in your mind's eye for about ten seconds**

- The Spanish for **soup** is **sopa**. (SOPA)
  Imagine a soup that tastes like **soap**.

- The Spanish for **rice** is **arroz**. (ARROS)
  Imagine someone shooting **arrows** that land in
  your plate of rice.

- The Spanish for **onion** is **cebolla**. (SEBOLYA)
  Imagine one onion turning to another and
  saying, "**They boil you** in this place."

- The Spanish for **mushroom** is **seta**. (SETA)
  Imagine being told to **say ta** by your mother,
  when she gives you a mushroom.

- The Spanish for **tomato** is **tomate**. (TOMATAY)
  Imagine throwing **tomatoes** at a bullfighter.

- The Spanish for **cheese** is **queso**. (KESO)
  Imagine a **case o'** cheese.

- The Spanish for **egg** is **huevo**. (HOO EVO)
  Imagine you give a **wave o** to someone who
  throws eggs at you.

- The Spanish for **water** is (el) **agua**. (AGOO A)
  Imagine an **aqueduct** bringing water to your hotel.

- The Spanish for **sugar** is **azúcar**. (ASOOKAR)
  Imagine stuffing **a cigar** into the sugar bowl.

- The Spanish for **coffee** is **café**. (KAFAY)
  Imagine drinking coffee in a **café**.

Please note: *Agua* is a "funny" word; it is *el agua*. It is a feminine word
that takes *el* for *the*.

131

☐ *You can write your answers in*

- What is the English for **café**?   _____

- What is the English for **azúcar**?   _____

- What is the English for (el) **agua**?   _____

- What is the English for **huevo**?   _____

- What is the English for **queso**?   _____

- What is the English for **tomate**?   _____

- What is the English for **seta**?   _____

- What is the English for **cebolla**?   _____

- What is the English for **arroz**?   _____

- What is the English for **sopa**?   _____

← *Look back for the answers*

☐ *You can write your answers in*

- What is the Spanish for **coffee**? _____

- What is the Spanish for **sugar**? _____

- What is the Spanish for **water**? _____

- What is the Spanish for **egg**? _____

- What is the Spanish for **cheese**? _____

- What is the Spanish for **tomato**? _____

- What is the Spanish for **mushroom**? _____

- What is the Spanish for **onion**? _____

- What is the Spanish for **rice**? _____

- What is the Spanish for **soup**? _____

← *Look back for the answers*

MORE FOOD AND DRINK WORDS

☐ **Think of each image in your mind's eye for about ten seconds**

* The Spanish for **bread** is **pan.** (PAN)
  Imagine loaves of bread stuffed in a **pan.**

* The Spanish for **meat** is (la) **carne.** (KARNAY)
  Imagine **carnivores** eating meat.

* The Spanish for **cauliflower** is (la) **coliflor.** (KOLEEFLOR)
  Imagine throwing a **cauliflower** at a bullfighter.

* The Spanish for **potato** is **papa.** (PAPA)
  Imagine throwing potatoes at your **Papa.**

* The Spanish for **wine** is **vino.** (VEENO)
  Imagine a German saying, "**Ve know** what a
  good wine it is."

* The Spanish for **milk** is (la) **leche.** (LECHAY)
  Imagine **leeches** in the milk.

* The Spanish for **beer** is **cerveza.** (SERVESA)
  Imagine demanding **service** for your beer
  in a bar.

* The Spanish for **pear** is **pera.** (PERA)
  Imagine buying a **pair a** pears.

* The Spanish for **cake** is **pastel.** (PASTEL)
  Imagine a **pastel**-colored cake.

* The Spanish for **cabbage** is (la) **col.** (KOL)
  Imagine you **call** someone a cabbage.

☐ *You can write your answers in*

- What is the English for (la) **col**? _____

- What is the English for **pastel**? _____

- What is the English for **pera**? _____

- What is the English for **cerveza**? _____

- What is the English for (la) **leche**? _____

- What is the English for **vino**? _____

- What is the English for **papa**? _____

- What is the English for (la) **coliflor**? _____

- What is the English for (la) **carne**? _____

- What is the English for **pan**? _____

← *Look back for the answers*

☐ *You can write your answers in*

- What is the Spanish for **cabbage**? _____

- What is the Spanish for **cake**? _____

- What is the Spanish for **pear**? _____

- What is the Spanish for **beer**? _____

- What is the Spanish for **milk**? _____

- What is the Spanish for **wine**? _____

- What is the Spanish for **potato**? _____

- What is the Spanish for **cauliflower**? _____

- What is the Spanish for **meat**? _____

- What is the Spanish for **bread**? _____

← *Look back for the answers*

SOME MORE USEFUL WORDS

☐ **Think of each image in your mind's eye for about ten seconds**

- The Spanish for **high** is **alto.** (ALTO)
  Imagine flying at a high **altitude.**

- The Spanish for **long** is **largo.** (LARGO)
  Imagine a long drink of lager.

- The Spanish for **expensive** is **caro.** (KARO)
  Imagine buying an expensive **car.**

- The Spanish for **cheap** is **barato.** (BARATO)
  Imagine a Spanish **baritone** going cheap at
  auction.

- The Spanish for **dirty** is **sucio.** (SOOSYO)
  Imagine you **soothe** your child, who is very
  dirty.

- The Spanish for **right** is **correcto.** (KORREKTO)
  Imagine something is **correct** and right.

- The Spanish for **wrong** is **incorrecto.** (EENKORREKTO)
  Imagine something is wrong and **incorrect.**

- The Spanish for **easy** is **fácil.** (FASEEL)
  Imagine someone has a **facility** for making
  things look easy.

- The Spanish for **angry** is **enojado.** (ENOHADO)
  Imagine someone being angry and **annoyed**
  with us.

☐ *You can write your answers in*

- What is the English for **fácil**? _____

- What is the English for **incorrecto**? _____

- What is the English for **correcto**? _____

- What is the English for **sucio**? _____

- What is the English for **barato**? _____

- What is the English for **caro**? _____

- What is the English for **largo**? _____

- What is the English for **alto**? _____

- What is the English for **enojado**? _____

← *Look back for the answers*

☐ *You can write your answers in*

- What is the Spanish for **easy**? _____

- What is the Spanish for **wrong**? _____

- What is the Spanish for **right**? _____

- What is the Spanish for **dirty**? _____

- What is the Spanish for **cheap**? _____

- What is the Spanish for **expensive**? _____

- What is the Spanish for **long**? _____

- What is the Spanish for **high**? _____

- What is the Spanish for **angry**? _____

← *Look back for the answers*

ELEMENTARY GRAMMAR

The Spanish for *was* is *estaba* when you use phrases like the following:

- *The pig was quick* is *El puerco estaba rápido*

- *The dog was dirty* is *El perro estaba sucio*

- *The cow was quiet* is *La vaca estaba tranquila*

The Spanish for *were* is *estaban* when you use phrases like the following:

- *The pigs were quick* is *Los puercos estaban rápidos*

- *The bulls were cheap* is *Los toros estaban baratos*

- *The frogs were dirty* is *Las ranas estaban sucias*

□ **Now cover up the answers below and translate the following:**

□ *(You can write your answers in)*

1. The red onions were very dirty.

2. The pigs and the ducks were angry.

3. The tomatoes were pretty.

4. The pears were cheap.

5. The cauliflower and the cabbage were dirty.

_____

_____

_____

_____

_____

_____

_____

_____

□ *The answers are:*

1. Las cebollas rojas estaban muy sucias.

2. Los puercos y los patos estaban enojados.

3. Los tomates estaban bonitos.

4. Las peras estaban baratas.

5. La coliflor y la col estaban sucias.

Now cover up the answers below and translate the following:

(You can write your answers in)

1. El arroz estaba sucio.

2. El menú estaba correcto.

3. Los quesos estaban frescos.

4. El menú estaba incorrecto.

5. Las setas estaban altas.

_____

_____

_____

_____

_____

_____

_____

☐ *The answers are:*

1. The rice was dirty.

2. The menu was right.

3. The cheeses were fresh.

4. The menu was wrong.

5. The mushrooms were high.

SOME MORE USEFUL WORDS

☐ **Think of each image in your mind's eye for about ten seconds**

- The Spanish for **first** is **primero**. (PREEMERO)
  Imagine being in the first, the **prime** position.

- The Spanish for **last** is **último**. (OOLTEEMO)
  Imagine getting an **ultimatum** for the last time.

- The Spanish for **here** is **aquí**. (AKEE)
  Imagine leaving **a key** here.

- The Spanish for **there** is **allá**. (ALYA)
  Imagine shouting, "Are you there—**all o' ya?**"

- The Spanish for **second** is **segundo**. (SEGOONDO)
  Imagine a bullfighter being the **second** person
  into the ring.

Note: *Primero* and *último* usually come before the noun as in English.
For example, *the first cow* is *la primera vaca*.

☐ *You can write your answers in*

- What is the English for **segundo**? _____

- What is the English for **allá**? _____

- What is the English for **aquí**? _____

- What is the English for **último**? _____

- What is the English for **primero**? _____

← *Look back for the answers*

☐ *You can write your answers in*

- What is the Spanish for **second**? _____

- What is the Spanish for **there**? _____

- What is the Spanish for **here**? _____

- What is the Spanish for **last**? _____

- What is the Spanish for **first**? _____

← *Look back for the answers*

□ **Now cover up the answers below and translate the following:**

□ *(You can write your answers in)*

1. The soup and the milk were here.

2. The water was here but the beer was there.

3. The last egg is here.

4. The coffee and the cake were here.

5. The meat is here and the bread is there.

_____

_____

_____

_____

_____

_____

_____

□ *The answers are:*

1. La sopa y la leche estaban aquí.

2. El agua estaba aquí pero la cerveza estaba allá.

3. El último huevo está aquí.

4. El café y el pastel estaban aquí.

5. La carne está aquí y el pan está allá.

148

☐ **Now cover up the answers below and translate the following:**

☐ *(You can write your answers in)*

1. Es la primera vaca.

2. Está aquí.

3. Está allá.

4. Es el último tomate.

5. Es la segunda cebolla.

_____

_____

_____

_____

_____

_____

_____

☐ *The answers are:*

1. It is the first cow.

2. She is here (or he, it).

3. He is there (or she, it).

4. It is the last tomato.

5. It is the second onion.

SECTION 7

SHOPPING AND BUSINESS WORDS

BUSINESS WORDS

☐ **Think of each image in your mind's eye for about ten seconds**

- The Spanish for **owner** is **propietario.**   (PROPEE ETARYO)
  Imagine asking to see the **proprietor,**
  the owner of a business.

- The Spanish for **manager** is **director.**   (DEEREKTOR)
  Imagine asking to see the manager, and the
  board of **directors** being brought to see you.

- The Spanish for **boss** is **jefe.**   (HEFAY)
  Imagine your boss behaves like the **chief.**

- The Spanish for **job** is **empleo.**   (EMPLEO)
  Imagine being **employed** to do a job.

- The Spanish for **factory** is **fábrica.**   (FABREEKA)
  Imagine a factory making **fabrics.**

- The Spanish for **salary** is **salario.**   (SALARYO)
  Imagine a bullfighter collecting a **salary.**

- The Spanish for **product** is **producto.**   (PRODOOKTO)
  Imagine selling a bullfighter your factory's
  product.

- The Spanish for **business** is **negocio.**   (NEGOSYO)
  Imagine having to **negotiate** for your business
  to be successful.

- The Spanish for **check** is **cheque.**   (CHEKAY)
  Imagine a bullfighter waving a **check** around.

- The Spanish for **office** is **oficina.**   (OFEESEENA)
  Imagine a bullfighter sitting in a big **office,**
  behind the desk.

151

- What is the English for **oficina**?   _____
- What is the English for **cheque**?   _____
- What is the English for **negocio**?   _____
- What is the English for **producto**?   _____
- What is the English for **salario**?   _____
- What is the English for **fábrica**?   _____
- What is the English for **empleo**?   _____
- What is the English for **jefe**?   _____
- What is the English for **director**?   _____
- What is the English for **propietario**?   _____

← *Look back for the answers*

☐ *You can write your answers in*

- What is the Spanish for **office**?   _____

- What is the Spanish for **check**?   _____

- What is the Spanish for **business**?   _____

- What is the Spanish for **product**?   _____

- What is the Spanish for **salary**?   _____

- What is the Spanish for **factory**?   _____

- What is the Spanish for **job**?   _____

- What is the Spanish for **boss**?   _____

- What is the Spanish for **manager**?   _____

- What is the Spanish for **owner**?   _____

← *Look back for the answers*

MORE BUSINESS WORDS

☐ **Think of each image in your mind's eye for about ten seconds**

- The Spanish for **receipt** is **recibo.**   (RESEEBO)
  Imagine getting a **receipt** from a bullfighter.

- The Spanish for **thing** is **cosa.**   (KOSA)
  Imagine asking if that thing **cost a** lot.

- The Spanish for **vacation** (holidays) is   (VAKASYONAYS)
  (las) **vacaciones.**
  Imagine a bullfighter who is going on **vacation.**

- The Spanish for **price** is **precio.**   (PRESYO)
  Imagine telling a street vendor, "I **praise you**
  for your low price."

- The Spanish for **mistake** is **error.**   (ERROR)
  Imagine a bullfighter making a bad **error.**

- The Spanish for **market** is **mercado.**   (MERKADO)
  Imagine a bullfighter buying goods in a
  market.

- The Spanish for **shop** is **tienda.**   (TEE ENDA)
  Imagine feeling **tender** as you enter a shop to
  buy your loved one something.

- The Spanish for **salesperson** is **vendedor.**   (VENDEDOR)
  Imagine a salesperson who **bends a door** in
  order to get into a business.

- The Spanish for **accountant** is **contador.**   (KONTADOR)
  Imagine an accountant sitting in an office,
  counting doors instead of money.

- The Spanish for **money** is **dinero.**   (DEENERO)
  Imagine using your money to buy your last
  dinner.

- What is the English for **dinero**? _____

- What is the English for **contador**? _____

- What is the English for **vendedor**? _____

- What is the English for **tienda**? _____

- What is the English for **mercado**? _____

- What is the English for **error**? _____

- What is the English for **precio**? _____

- What is the English for (las) **vacaciones**? _____

- What is the English for **cosa**? _____

- What is the English for **recibo**? _____

← *Look back for the answers*

156

☐ *You can write your answers in*

- What is the Spanish for **money**?   _____

- What is the Spanish for **accountant**?   _____

- What is the Spanish for **salesperson**?   _____

- What is the Spanish for **shop**?   _____

- What is the Spanish for **market**?   _____

- What is the Spanish for **mistake**?   _____

- What is the Spanish for **price**?   _____

- What is the Spanish for **vacation**?   _____

- What is the Spanish for **thing**?   _____

- What is the Spanish for **receipt**?   _____

← *Look back for the answers*

SOME MORE USEFUL WORDS

☐ **Think of each image in your mind's eye for about ten seconds**

- The Spanish for **where** is **dónde.**   (DONDAY)
  Imagine asking, "*Where* on earth is **Dundee?**"

- The Spanish for **why** is **por qué.**   (POR KAY)
  Imagine asking your mother, "*Why* **pork** for tea
  again?"

- The Spanish for **how** is **cómo.**   (KOMO)
  Imagine asking, "*How* **come?**"

- The Spanish for **who** is **quién.**   (KEE EN)
  Imagine an ignorant person asking, "*Who* is the
  queen?"

- The Spanish for **how much** is **cuánto.**   (KOO ANTO)
  Imagine asking *how much* it is when you buy a
  large **quantity.**

☐ *You can write your answers in*

- What is the English for **cuánto?** _____

- What is the English for **quién?** _____

- What is the English for **cómo?** _____

- What is the English for **por qué?** _____

- What is the English for **dónde?** _____

← *Look back for the answers*

☐ *You can write your answers in*

- What is the Spanish for **how much**? _____

- What is the Spanish for **who**? _____

- What is the Spanish for **how**? _____

- What is the Spanish for **why**? _____

- What is the Spanish for **where**? _____

← *Look back for the answers*

161

ELEMENTARY GRAMMAR

When you ask questions using words like *where* or *why,* you ask a question in the same way as in English.

→ *For example:*

- *¿Por qué quiere un animal?* is *Why does he* (or *she*) *want an animal?*

- *¿Dónde está el mercado?*   is *Where is the market?*

- *¿Cómo come el pato?*   is *How does he (or she) eat the duck?*

- *¿Quién es la muchacha?*   is *Who is the girl?*

When you want to say *you* (for example, *you eat*) in Spanish, you do not need the word for *you.*

So, in Spanish, *you eat* is the same as *eats (come).*

- *you want* is *wants (quiere)*

- *you have* is *has (tiene)*

Remember that you also do not need the words for *he, she, it,* etc.

162

☐ **Now cover up the answers below and translate the following:**

☐ *(You can write your answers in)*

1. Who is the owner?

2. Where is the manager?

3. Why is the boy quick?

4. How do you want the duck?

5. How much money has he?

_____

_____

_____

_____

_____

_____

_____

☐ *The answers are:*

1. ¿Quién es el propietario?

2. ¿Dónde está el director?

3. ¿Por qué el muchacho está rápido?

4. ¿Cómo quiere el pato?

5. ¿Cuánto dinero tiene?

163

☐ **Now cover up the answers below and translate the following:**

☐ *(You can write your answers in)*

1. ¿Dónde están el propietario y el director?

2. ¿Por qué están los jefes y los directores sucios?

3. ¿Cómo quiere (= you) las tiendas y las fábricas?

4. ¿Cuánto es el salario?

5. ¿Por qué están sucios los cheques y los recibos?

_____

_____

_____

_____

_____

☐ *The answers are:*

1. Where are the owner and the manager?

2. Why are the bosses and the managers dirty?

3. How do you want the shops and the factories?

4. How much is the salary?

5. Why are the checks and the receipts dirty?

Remember, the word order is not changed in Spanish when you ask a question.

Don't worry if you make mistakes. You will be understood.

BUSINESSES AND SHOPS

☐ **Think of each image in your mind's eye for about ten seconds**

- The Spanish for **barber's shop** is **barbería.** (BARBEREE A)
  Imagine that the barber who is cutting your hair
  is a **barbarian.**

- The Spanish for **pharmacy** is **farmacia.** (FARMASYA)
  Imagine a bullfighter in a **pharmacy.**

- The Spanish for **hardware store** is (FERRETEREE A)
  ferretería.
  Imagine **ferrets** running wild in a hardware
  store.

- The Spanish for **laundromat** is **lavandería.** (LAVANDEREE A)
  Imagine someone spilling **lavender** water
  all over the laundromat.

- The Spanish for **supermarket** is (SOOPER MERKADO)
  supermercado.
  Imagine bullfighters doing their weekly
  shopping in a **supermarket.**

- The Spanish for **tobacco shop** (tobacconist) (TABAKEREE A)
  is **tabaquería.**
  Imagine a bullfighter in a **tobacco shop.**

☐ *You can write your answers in*

- What is the English for **tabaquería?** _____

- What is the English for **supermercado?** _____

- What is the English for **lavandería?** _____

- What is the English for **ferretería?** _____

- What is the English for **farmacia?** _____

- What is the English for **barbería?** _____

← *Look back for the answers*

166

☐ *You can write your answers in*

- What is the Spanish for **tobacco shop**? _____

- What is the Spanish for **supermarket**? _____

- What is the Spanish for **laundromat**? _____

- What is the Spanish for **hardware store**? _____

- What is the Spanish for **pharmacy**? _____

- What is the Spanish for **barber's shop**? _____

← *Look back for the answers*

☐ **Now cover up the answers below and translate the following:**

☐ *(You can write your answers in)*

1. The supermarket and the pharmacy are here.

2. The salesperson wants a receipt and the money.

3. The accountant has a job in the office.

4. The barber's shop and the laundromat are good businesses.

5. The mistake is here.

_____

_____

_____

_____

_____

_____

☐ *The answers are:*

1. El supermercado y la farmacia están aquí.

2. El vendedor quiere un recibo y el dinero.

3. El contador tiene un empleo en la oficina.

4. La barbería y la lavandería son buenos negocios.
   (Note: *Good* often comes before the noun.)

5. El error está aquí.

□ **Now cover up the answers below and translate the following:**

□ *(You can write your answers in)*

1. Las farmacias están aquí y no allá.

2. Los productos son muy buenos.

3. El precio es siempre alto.

4. La ferretería tiene cosas caras.

5. La primera tienda es muy larga.

_____

_____

_____

_____

_____

_____

_____

□ *The answers are:*

1. The pharmacies are here and not there.

2. The products are very good.

3. The price is always high.

4. The hardware store has expensive things.

5. The first shop is very long.

SECTION 8

TRAVELING, THE CAR

TRAVELING AND ARRIVING AT YOUR DESTINATION

☐ **Think of each image in your mind's eye for about ten seconds**

- The Spanish for **passport** is **pasaporte.** (PASAPORTAY)
  Imagine a bullfighter stamping your **passport**
  when you arrive in Spain.

- The Spanish for **suitcase** is **maleta.** (MALETA)
  Imagine **my letter** is in your suitcase.

- The Spanish for **customs** is **aduana.** (ADOO ANA)
  Imagine going through the customs saying,
  "**Add one.** Add two," etc.

- The Spanish for **bathroom** is (QUARTO DAY BANYO)
  cuarto de baño.
  Imagine, if you have no **quarter, they ban you**
  from the bathroom.

- The Spanish for **ticket** is **billete.** (BEELYETAY)
  Imagine thinking "I will **be late** if I don't find
  my tickets."

- The Spanish for **danger** is **peligro.** (PELEEGRO)
  Imagine someone shouting, "Danger, don't eat
  that. It will make your **belly grow.**"

- The Spanish for **gentlemen** is **señores.** (SENYORAYS)
  Imagine a number of **senior** men entering the
  library.

- The Spanish for **ladies** is **señoras.** (SENYORAS)
  Imagine a number of **senior** ladies entering the
  library.

- The Spanish for **entrance** is **entrada.** (ENTRADA)
  Imagine a bullfighter **entering a** bullring.

- The Spanish for **exit** is **salida.** (SALEEDA)
  Imagine **salad** spread all over the exit to your
  hotel.

171

☐ *You can write your answers in*

- What is the English for **salida**? _____

- What is the English for **entrada**? _____

- What is the English for **señoras**? _____

- What is the English for **señores**? _____

- What is the English for **peligro**? _____

- What is the English for **billete**? _____

- What is the English for **cuarto de baño**? _____

- What is the English for **aduana**? _____

- What is the English for **maleta**? _____

- What is the English for **pasaporte**? _____

← *Look back for the answers*

☐ *You can write your answers in*

- What is the Spanish for **exit**?   _____

- What is the Spanish for **entrance**?   _____

- What is the Spanish for **ladies**?   _____

- What is the Spanish for **gentlemen**?   _____

- What is the Spanish for **danger**?   _____

- What is the Spanish for **ticket**?   _____

- What is the Spanish for **bathroom**?   _____

- What is the Spanish for **customs**?   _____

- What is the Spanish for **suitcase**?   _____

- What is the Spanish for **passport**?   _____

← *Look back for the answers*

MORE TRAVELING WORDS

☐ **Think of each image in your mind's eye for about ten seconds**

- The Spanish for **boat** is **barco**.   (BARKO)
  Imagine a dog **barking** as you embark on a boat.

- The Spanish for **car** is **carro**.   (KARRO)
  Imagine saying, "My **car, oh!**"

- The Spanish for **bus** is **autobús**.   (A OOTOBOOS)
  Imagine **a bus** filled with bullfighters.

- The Spanish for **train** is **tren**.   (TREN)
  Imagine bullfighters leaning out of **train** carriages.

- The Spanish for **garage** is **garaje**.   (GARAHAY)
  Imagine a bullfighter pumping gas in front of a
  garage.

- The Spanish for **gas** is **gasolina**.   (GASOLEENA)
  Imagine a bullfighter pumping **gasoline**.

- The Spanish for **flat tire** is **pinchazo**.   (PEENCHASO)
  Imagine a finger you **pinch as you** change
  a flat tire.

- The Spanish for **flat tire** is **pinchazo**.   (PEENCHASO)
  Imagine a finger you **punch as you** change a
  flat tire.

- The Spanish for **wheel** is **rueda**.   (ROO EDA)
  Imagine little wheels appearing on a **radar**
  screen.

- The Spanish for **jack** is **gato**.   (GATO)
  Imagine saying, "I **got'o** have a jack to change
  my tire."
  (It's the same as for *cat*.)

175

☐ *You can write your answers in*

- What is the English for **gato**? _____

- What is the English for **rueda**? _____

- What is the English for **pinchazo**? _____

- What is the English for **aceite**? _____

- What is the English for **gasolina**? _____

- What is the English for **garaje**? _____

- What is the English for **tren**? _____

- What is the English for **autobús**? _____

- What is the English for **carro**? _____

- What is the English for **barco**? _____

← *Look back for the answers*

☐ *You can write your answers in*

- What is the Spanish for **jack**?   _____

- What is the Spanish for **wheel**?   _____

- What is the Spanish for **flat tire**?   _____

- What is the Spanish for **oil**?   _____

- What is the Spanish for **gasoline**?   _____

- What is the Spanish for **garage**?   _____

- What is the Spanish for **train**?   _____

- What is the Spanish for **bus**?   _____

- What is the Spanish for **car**?   _____

- What is the Spanish for **boat**?   _____

← *Look back for the answers*

ELEMENTARY GRAMMAR

You will remember that the Spanish for

- *eats* is *come*

- *has* is *tiene*

- *wants* is *quiere*

  - The Spanish for *I want* is *quiero* (pronounced KEE ERO)

  - The Spanish for *I eat* is *como* (pronounced KOMO)

  - The Spanish for *I have* is *tengo* (pronounced TENGO)

Remember that for I, use *o* at the end of the word.

➡ *So,*

- *I have a ticket* is *Tengo un billete*

Note that in Spanish *I want* and *I am wanting*, *I eat* and *I am eating*, etc., are the same.

☐ **Now cover up the answers below and translate the following:**

☐ *(You can write your answers in)*

1. I have a ticket.

2. I want the customs.

3. I am eating the pig.

4. He is the boss.

5. I have a boat and a car.

_____

_____

_____

_____

_____

_____

_____

☐ *The answers are:*

1. Tengo un billete.

2. Quiero la aduana.

3. Como el puerco.

4. Es el jefe.

5. Tengo un barco y un carro.

☐ **Now cover up the answers below and translate the following:**

☐ *(You can write your answers in)*

1. Es el propietario.

2. Tengo un pasaporte y una maleta.

3. Como el billete, y el perro come la rueda.

4. Quiero un garaje.

5. Es el contador.

_____

_____

_____

_____

_____

_____

_____

_____

☐ *The answers are:*

1. He is the owner (or You are the owner).

2. I have a passport and a suitcase.

3. I am eating the ticket, and the dog is eating the wheel.

4. I want a garage.

5. He is the accountant (or You are the accountant).

ELEMENTARY GRAMMAR

The next elementary grammar point is about the word for *I am*.

In Spanish, the phrase *I am* is *estoy* if the state is temporary or *soy* if it is permanent.

→ *For example:*

Permanent State	Temporary State
I am a pig	I am angry
Soy un puerco	Estoy enojado
I am a dog	I am dirty
Soy un perro	Estoy sucio
I am the manager	I am free
Soy el director	Estoy libre

In an earlier section, you learned that the word for *no* is *no*, and it is also the word for *not*.

To say *The car is not small*, you simply say *The car not is small*:

* *El carro no es pequeño*

In other words, you put the *no* before the verb.

→ *So,*

* *The dog is not quick* is *El perro no es rápido*

181

There is one important rule to remember: the word for *a* is usually omitted when you use the word *no*.

→ *For example:*

• *I do not have a cow* is *No tengo vaca*

(Remember *I* is left out in Spanish.)

• *You do not have a bull* is *No tiene toro*

• *You do not eat pigs*   is *No come puercos*

• *I am a dog*   is *Soy un perro*

• *I am not a dog*   is *No soy perro*

For the word *the*, *el* or *la* are left in.

• *I am not the pig* is *No soy el puerco*

☐ **Now cover up the answers below and translate the following:**

☐ *(You can write your answers in)*

1. It is not the car.

2. He is not a duck.

3. I am not the owner.

4. I have a passport.

5. It is not a suitcase.

_____

_____

_____

_____

_____

_____

☐ *The answers are:*

1. No es el carro.

2. No es pato.

3. No soy el propietario.

4. Tengo un pasaporte.

5. No es maleta.

☐ **Now cover up the answers below and translate the following:**

☐ *(You can write your answers in)*

1. Estoy sucio. El cuarto de baño está aquí.

2. Soy pequeño, pero como un caballo.

3. La cama es dura y vieja.

4. Tengo una maleta amarilla, y la muchacha tiene una maleta azul.

5. Soy un marido, y quiero sopa o leche y azúcar.

_____

_____

_____

_____

_____

_____

_____

☐ *The answers are:*

1. I am dirty. The bathroom is here.

2. I am small, but I eat a horse.

3. The bed is hard and old.

4. I have a yellow suitcase, and the girl has a blue suitcase.

5. I am a husband, and I want soup or milk and sugar.

SOME MORE TRAVELING WORDS

☐ **Think of each image in your mind's eye for about ten seconds**

- The Spanish for **tire** is **neumático.**   (NE OOMATEEKO)
  Imagine blowing up a **pneumatic** tire.

- The Spanish for **exhaust** is **escape.**   (ESCAPAY)
  Imagine exhaust fumes **escaping** from a car.

- The Spanish for **map** is (el) **mapa.**   (MAPA)
  Imagine a bullfighter studying a **map.**

- The Spanish for **pump** is **bomba.**   (BOMBA)
  Imagine a **bomb** on your pump, which explodes
  when the pump is switched on.

- The Spanish for **key** is (la) **llave.**   (LYAVAY)
  Imagine that you have left your key in the
  lavatory.

- The Spanish for **engine** is **motor.**   (MOTOR)
  Imagine your **motor** car won't start because the
  engine has broken down.

- The Spanish for **driver** is **conductor.**   (KONDOOKTOR)
  Imagine the driver of your car is a bus
  conductor.

- The Spanish for **fan** is **ventilador.**   (VENTEELADOR)
  Imagine you use a fan for a **ventilator** for
  your car.

- The Spanish for **seat** is **asiento.**   (ASEE ENTO)
  Imagine you have to **ascend to** sit on your seat.

- The Spanish for **tank** is **depósito.**   (DEPOSEETO)
  Imagine you **deposit** gas in your tank.

☐ *You can write your answers in*

- What is the English for **depósito**? _____
- What is the English for **asiento**? _____
- What is the English for **ventilador**? _____
- What is the English for **conductor**? _____
- What is the English for **motor**? _____
- What is the English for (la) **llave**? _____
- What is the English for **bomba**? _____
- What is the English for (el) **mapa**? _____
- What is the English for **escape**? _____
- What is the English for **neumático**? _____

← *Look back for the answers*

☐ *You can write your answers in*

- What is the Spanish for **tank**? _____

- What is the Spanish for **seat**? _____

- What is the Spanish for **fan**? _____

- What is the Spanish for **driver**? _____

- What is the Spanish for **engine**? _____

- What is the Spanish for **key**? _____

- What is the Spanish for **pump**? _____

- What is the Spanish for **map**? _____

- What is the Spanish for **exhaust**? _____

- What is the Spanish for **tire**? _____

← *Look back for the answers*

ELEMENTARY GRAMMAR

The Spanish for *some* is *unos* or *unas*.

- *unos* is *masculine*

- *unas* is *feminine*

➔ *So,*

- *Tengo unas vacas* is *I have some cows*

- *Como unos toros* is *I eat some bulls*

☐ **Now cover up the answers below and translate the following:**

☐ *(You can write your answers in)*

1. I have some tickets.

2. I eat some cats.

3. I want some wheels.

4. She has some tables.

5. It has some geese.

_____

_____

_____

_____

_____

_____

_____

_____

☐ *The answers are:*

1. Tengo unos billetes.

2. Como unos gatos.

3. Quiero unas ruedas.

4. Tiene unas mesas.

5. Tiene unos gansos.

189

□ **Now cover up the answers below and translate the following:**

□ *(You can write your answers in)*

1. No es entrada y no es salida.

2. Quiere (= he) unos pasaportes pero no el billete.

3. No, no es la aduana.

4. Los señores y las señoras están aquí.

5. El autobús, el carro y el tren están en el garaje.

_____

_____

_____

_____

_____

_____

_____

□ *The answers are:*

1. It is not an entrance and it is not an exit.

2. He wants some passports but not the ticket.

3. No, it is not the customs.

4. The gentlemen and the ladies are here.

5. The bus, the car, and the train are in the garage.

ELEMENTARY GRAMMAR

To say you do *not* have some cows, or tables, and so on, you leave out the *unos* and *unas*.

- *No tengo maletas* is *I do not have (any) suitcases*

- *No como patos* is *I do not eat (any) ducks*

☐ **Now cover up the answers below and translate the following:**

☐ *(You can write your answers in)*

1. You do not want (any) tickets.

2. He does not eat (any) plates.

3. You do not have (any) passports.

4. She has some cars.

5. I do not have (any) suitcases.

_____

_____

_____

_____

_____

_____

_____

_____

☐ *The answers are:*

1. No quiere billetes.

2. No come platos.

3. No tiene pasaportes.

4. Tiene unos carros.

5. No tengo maletas.

192

☐ Now cover up the answers below and translate the following:

☐ *(You can write your answers in)*

1. Es un pinchazo pero no tengo gato.

2. El conductor quiere gasolina y aceite en el depósito.

3. Los neumáticos son muy viejos.

4. No quiero ruedas, no quiero bombas pero quiero unos asientos y unos ventiladores.

5. No tengo barcos amarillos.

_____

_____

_____

_____

_____

_____

☐ *The answers are:*

1. It is a flat tire but I do not have a jack.

2. The driver wants gas and oil in the tank.

3. The tires are very old.

4. I do not want (any) wheels, I do not want (any) pumps, but I want some seats and some fans.

5. I do not have (any) yellow boats.

193

SECTION 9

LEISURE ACTIVITIES

☐ **Think of each image in your mind's eye for about ten seconds**

- The Spanish for **beach** is **playa.**   (PLAYA)
  Imagine you **play a** game on the beach.

- The Spanish for **sand** is **arena.**   (ARENA)
  Imagine clowns in a circus **arena** throwing sand
  at each other.

- The Spanish for **deck chair** is **hamaca.**   (AMAKA)
  Imagine a **hammock** slung between two deck
  chairs.

- The Spanish for **picnic** is **merienda.**   (MEREE ENDA)
  Imagine your picnic coming to a **merry end,**
  possibly because people have drunk too much.

- The Spanish for **sun** is **sol.**   (SOL)
  Imagine **Saul** in the Bible, staring at the sun.

- The Spanish for **cold** is **frío.**   (FREE O)
  Imagine being **free**zing cold.

- The Spanish for **heat** is **calor.**   (KALOR)
  Imagine the heat is making you a funny **color.**

- The Spanish for (to) **rescue** is **salvar.**   (SALVAR)
  Imagine giving someone a silver **salver** after the
  person has rescued you.

- The Spanish for **sea** is **mar.**   (MAR)
  Imagine yelling, "**Ma!** Get me out of the sea."

- The Spanish for **rock** is **roca.**   (ROKA)
  Imagine a bullfighter standing on some **rocks.**

- What is the English for **roca**? _____

- What is the English for **mar**? _____

- What is the English for **salvar**? _____

- What is the English for **calor**? _____

- What is the English for **frío**? _____

- What is the English for **sol**? _____

- What is the English for **merienda**? _____

- What is the English for **hamaca**? _____

- What is the English for **arena**? _____

- What is the English for **playa**? _____

← *Look back for the answers*

☐ *You can write your answers in*

- What is the Spanish for **rock**? _____
- What is the Spanish for **sea**? _____
- What is the Spanish for **to rescue**? _____
- What is the Spanish for **heat**? _____
- What is the Spanish for **cold**? _____
- What is the Spanish for **sun**? _____
- What is the Spanish for **picnic**? _____
- What is the Spanish for **deck chair**? _____
- What is the Spanish for **sand**? _____
- What is the Spanish for **beach**? _____

← *Look back for the answers*

197

ELEMENTARY GRAMMAR

Here are some useful words:

☐ The Spanish for *my* is *mi* (pronounced MEE).

Imagine thinking "Give *me* my car."

☐ The Spanish for *your, his, her,* and *its* is *su* (pronounced SOO).

Imagine thinking, I will *sue* your, his, her, its family for damages.

➡ *So,*

- *my bull*　is *mi toro*

- *my cow*　is *mi vaca*

- *your beach* is *su playa*

- *His* or *her beach* is also *su playa.*

- *Its* (or *his* or *her* or *your*) *picnic* is *su merienda.*

☐ The Spanish for *my* and *your* when the noun is plural is *mis* or *sus*. In other words, you add an *s*.

➡ *So,*

- *my cows*　　is *mis vacas*

- *my tires*　　is *mis neumáticos*

- *my beaches*　is *mis playas*

- *your deck chairs* is *sus hamacas*

- *your picnics*　is *sus meriendas*

LEISURE ACTIVITIES

☐ **Think of each image in your mind's eye for about ten seconds**

- The Spanish for **party** is **fiesta.**   (FEE ESTA)
  Imagine having a **feast** in the middle of your
  party.

- The Spanish for **bullfight** is **corrida.**   (KORREEDA)
  Imagine having a bullfight in a **corridor.**

- The Spanish for **lake** is **lago.**   (LAGO)
  Imagine a lake with a **lack o'** water.

- The Spanish for **river** is **río.**   (REE O)
  Imagine a famous river, the **Rio** Grande.

- The Spanish for **mountain** is **montaña.**   (MONTANYA)
  Imagine mountains in the state of **Montana.**

- The Spanish for **stamp** is **sello.**   (SELYO)
  Imagine someone who wants to **sell you** a
  stamp.

- The Spanish for **envelope** is **sobre.**   (SOBRAY)
  Imagine being just **sober** enough to seal an
  envelope.

- The Spanish for **letter** is **carta.**   (KARTA)
  Imagine you put a letter in a go-**cart.**

- The Spanish for **pen** is **pluma.**   (PLOOMA)
  Imagine **pluma**ge sticking out of your pen.

- The Spanish for **book** is **libro.**   (LEEBRO)
  Imagine a **library** with books.

- What is the English for **libro**? _____
- What is the English for **pluma**? _____
- What is the English for **carta**? _____
- What is the English for **sobre**? _____
- What is the English for **sello**? _____
- What is the English for **montaña**? _____
- What is the English for **río**? _____
- What is the English for **lago**? _____
- What is the English for **corrida**? _____
- What is the English for **fiesta**? _____

← *Look back for the answers*

□ *You can write your answers in*

- What is the Spanish for **book**? _____

- What is the Spanish for **pen**? _____

- What is the Spanish for **letter**? _____

- What is the Spanish for **envelope**? _____

- What is the Spanish for **stamp**? _____

- What is the Spanish for **mountain**? _____

- What is the Spanish for **river**? _____

- What is the Spanish for **lake**? _____

- What is the Spanish for **bullfight**? _____

- What is the Spanish for **party**? _____

← *Look back for the answers*

☐ **Now cover up the answers below and translate the following:**

☐ *(You can write your answers in)*

1. I am your boy.

2. I am his brother.

3. It is my pig.

4. It is my beach.

5. It is my sun.

_____

_____

_____

_____

_____

_____

_____

☐ *The answers are:*

1. Soy su muchacho.
2. Soy su hermano.
3. Es mi puerco.
4. Es mi playa.
5. Es mi sol.

☐ **Now cover up the answers below and translate the following:**

☐ *(You can write your answers in)*

1. La arena está en sus hamacas y está en mis cartas.

2. Es su sobre, y mi sella.

3. Quiero sus montañas y sus ríos.

4. ¡Peligro! Su fiesta está muy tranquila.

5. El agua está fría hoy, pero la merienda está aquí en un barco en el lago.

Note: In written Spanish, an upside-down exclamation mark is used at the beginning of an exclamation.

_____

_____

_____

☐ *The answers are:*

1. The sand is on your (or his, her) deck chairs and is on (or in) my letters.

2. It is your (or his, her, its) envelope, and my stamp.

3. I want your (or his, her, its) mountains and your (or his, her, its) rivers.

4. Danger! Your (or his, her, its) party is very quiet.

5. The water is cold today, but the picnic is here on (or in) a boat on (or in) the lake.

Remember: *su* can be *your* or *his* or *her* or *its*.

203

SOME MORE USEFUL WORDS

☐ **Think of each image in your mind's eye for about ten seconds**

- The Spanish for **doctor** is **médico.** (MEDEEKO)
  Imagine your doctor with bottles of **medicine.**

- The Spanish for **dentist** is (el) **dentista.** (DENTEESTA)
  Imagine a bullfighter at the **dentist's.**

- The Spanish for **lawyer** is **abogado.** (ABOGADO)
  Imagine a lawyer eating an **avocado** in the
  middle of the defense of a client.

- The Spanish for **police** is **policía.** (POLEESEE A)
  Imagine the **police** arresting a bullfighter.

- The Spanish for **bank** is **banco.** (BANKO)
  Imagine your **bank** filled with bullfighters.

- The Spanish for **hotel** is **hotel.** (OTEL)
  Imagine a bullfighter's convention at your
  hotel.

- The Spanish for **post office** is **correo.** (KORREO)
  Imagine a post office in **Korea,** with Korean
  signs outside.

- The Spanish for **camping site** is **camping.** (CAMPEENG)
  Imagine bullfighters **camping** at a camping site.

- The Spanish for **road** is **carretera.** (KARRETERA)
  Imagine **carrots** strewn all over the road.

- The Spanish for **museum** is **museo.** (MOOSEO)
  Imagine an exhibition of bullfighters at your
  local **museum.**

☐ *You can write your answers in*

- What is the English for **museo**?   _____

- What is the English for **carretera**?   _____

- What is the English for **camping**?   _____

- What is the English for **correo**?   _____

- What is the English for **hotel**?   _____

- What is the English for **banco**?   _____

- What is the English for **policía**?   _____

- What is the English for (el) **abogado**?   _____

- What is the English for (el) **dentista**?   _____

- What is the English for **médico**?   _____

← *Look back for the answers*

☐ *You can write your answers in*

- What is the Spanish for **museum**? _____

- What is the Spanish for **road**? _____

- What is the Spanish for **camping site**? _____

- What is the Spanish for **post office**? _____

- What is the Spanish for **hotel**? _____

- What is the Spanish for **bank**? _____

- What is the Spanish for **police**? _____

- What is the Spanish for **lawyer**? _____

- What is the Spanish for **dentist**? _____

- What is the Spanish for **doctor**? _____

← *Look back for the answers*

□ **Now cover up the answers below and translate the following:**

□ *(You can write your answers in)*

1. The heat is here today.

2. The sea and the rock were here, but the road and the museum are not here.

3. The bullfight was in the hotel.

4. Your doctor wants more money and my dentist wants more cheese.

5. My dogs were under a bank.

_____

_____

_____

_____

_____

_____

□ *The answers are:*

1. El calor está aquí hoy.

2. El mar y la roca estaban aquí, pero la carretera y el museo no están aquí.

3. La corrida estaba en el hotel.

4. Su médico quiere más dinero y mi dentista quiere más queso.

5. Mis perros estaban debajo de un banco.

☐ **Now cover up the answers below and translate the following:**

☐ *(You can write your answers in)*

1. La pluma y el libro están en la mesa.

2. Mis abogados están fuera de un guardarropa.

3. La llave y el mapa estaban en la carretera.

4. Mi motor y mi escape son muy viejos.

5. El camping y el correo tienen flores azules.

_____

_____

_____

_____

_____

_____

_____

☐ *The answers are:*

1. The pen and the book are on the table.

2. My lawyers are outside a cloakroom.

3. The key and the map were on the road.

4. My engine and my exhaust are very old.

5. The camping site and the post office have blue flowers.

ELEMENTARY GRAMMAR

Verbs with plural subjects in sentences such as *The campsite and the post office have . . .* or *they have,* or *they eat,* etc., always end in *n.*

→ *So,*

- *The campsite and the post office* **have** *. . .* is
  El camping y el correo **tienen** *. . .*

- *The cows and the ducks* **want** *. . .* is
  Las vacas y los patos **quieren** *. . .*

SECTION 10

AT THE DOCTOR'S, EMERGENCY WORDS, USEFUL WORDS

ILLNESS

☐ **Think of each image in your mind's eye for about ten seconds**

* The Spanish for **pain** is **dolor.**   (DOLOR)
  Imagine being given a **dollar** to make your pain
  go away.

* The Spanish for **ill** is **enfermo.**   (ENFERMO)
  Imagine being ill and **infirm.**

* The Spanish for **cough** is (la) **tos.**   (TOS)
  Imagine you cough in the middle of **tossing** a
  coin, and drop the coin.

* The Spanish for **arm** is **brazo.**   (BRASO)
  Imagine **brass** bracelets wrapped around your
  arm.

* The Spanish for **eye** is **ojo.**   (OHO)
  Imagine the doctor saying, "**Oh ho!**" while
  poking you in the eye.

* The Spanish for **face** is **cara.**   (KARA)
  Imagine your face looking as if a **car had** hit it.

* The Spanish for **hand** is (la) **mano.**   (MANO)
  Imagine dropping someone's hand down a
  manhole.

* The Spanish for **skin** is (la) **piel.**   (PEE EL)
  Imagine your skin beginning to **peel** in the sun.

* The Spanish for **blood** is (la) **sangre.**   (SANGRAY)
  Imagine being **so angry** that you draw blood.

* The Spanish for **mouth** is (la) **boca.**   (BOKA)
  Imagine **a poker** sticking out of someone's
  mouth.

☐ *You can write your answers in*

- What is the English for **boca**?　　　＿＿＿＿＿＿＿

- What is the English for (la) **sangre**?　　＿＿＿＿＿＿＿

- What is the English for (la) **piel**?　　＿＿＿＿＿＿＿

- What is the English for (la) **mano**?　　＿＿＿＿＿＿＿

- What is the English for **cara**?　　＿＿＿＿＿＿＿

- What is the English for **ojo**?　　＿＿＿＿＿＿＿

- What is the English for **brazo**?　　＿＿＿＿＿＿＿

- What is the English for (la) **tos**?　　＿＿＿＿＿＿＿

- What is the English for **enfermo**?　　＿＿＿＿＿＿＿

- What is the English for **dolor**?　　＿＿＿＿＿＿＿

← *Look back for the answers*

☐ *You can write your answers in*

- What is the Spanish for **mouth**?   _____

- What is the Spanish for **blood**?   _____

- What is the Spanish for **skin**?   _____

- What is the Spanish for **hand**?   _____

- What is the Spanish for **face**?   _____

- What is the Spanish for **eye**?   _____

- What is the Spanish for **arm**?   _____

- What is the Spanish for **cough**?   _____

- What is the Spanish for **ill**?   _____

- What is the Spanish for **pain**?   _____

← *Look back for the answers*

EMERGENCY AND USEFUL WORDS

☐ **Think of each image in your mind's eye for about ten seconds**

- The Spanish for **hospital** is **hospital.**   (OSPEETAL)
  Imagine a bullfighter being carted off to a
  hospital.

- The Spanish for **bandage** is **venda.**   (VENDA)
  Imagine you **bend a** bandage backwards and
  forwards to get it off.

- The Spanish for **ambulance** is **ambulancia.** (AMBOOLANSYA)
  Imagine a bullfighter being loaded into an
  ambulance.

- The Spanish for **accident** is **accidente.**   (AKSEEDENTAY)
  Imagine a bullfighter in a nasty **accident.**

- The Spanish for **thief** is **ladrón.**   (LADRON)
  Imagine a thief disappearing down the street
  with a **ladder on** his back.

- The Spanish for **fire** is **fuego.**   (FOO EGO)
  Imagine telling the hotel manager, "**If we go,**
  there will be a fire."

- The Spanish for **dead** is **muerto.**   (MOO ERTO)
  Imagine telling people that they are **mortal,** that
  is why they are now dead.

- The Spanish for **street** is **(la) calle.**   (KALYAY)
  Imagine you hear someone **call you** in the
  street.

- The Spanish for **help** is **ayuda.**   (AYOODA)
  Imagine shouting, "**Hey, you there,** help!"

- The Spanish for **telephone** is **teléfono.**   (TELEFONO)
  Imagine a bullfighter using a **telephone.**

☐ *You can write your answers in*

- What is the English for **teléfono**? _____

- What is the English for **ayuda**? _____

- What is the English for (la) **calle**? _____

- What is the English for **muerto**? _____

- What is the English for **fuego**? _____

- What is the English for **ladrón**? _____

- What is the English for **accidente**? _____

- What is the English for **ambulancia**? _____

- What is the English for **venda**? _____

- What is the English for **hospital**? _____

← *Look back for the answers*

☐ *You can write your answers in*

- What is the Spanish for **telephone**?   _____

- What is the Spanish for **help**?   _____

- What is the Spanish for **street**?   _____

- What is the Spanish for **dead**?   _____

- What is the Spanish for **fire**?   _____

- What is the Spanish for **thief**?   _____

- What is the Spanish for **accident**?   _____

- What is the Spanish for **ambulance**?   _____

- What is the Spanish for **bandage**?   _____

- What is the Spanish for **hospital**?   _____

← *Look back for the answers*

MORE USEFUL WORDS

☐ **Think of each image in your mind's eye for about ten seconds**

- The Spanish for **thank you** is **gracias.**   (GRASYAS)
  Imagine someone being **gracious** and saying
  thank you.

- The Spanish for **please** is **por favor.**   (POR FAVOR)
  Imagine thinking, "Please **pour favors** in my
  direction."

- The Spanish for **sorry** is **perdone.**   (PERDONAY)
  Imagine saying, "**Pardon,** I am sorry."

- The Spanish for **hello** is **hola.**   (OLA)
  Imagine saying "hello" to someone who is
  practicing with a **hoola**-hoop.

- The Spanish for **good-bye** is **adiós.**   (ADYOS)
  Imagine thinking, "Good-bye, **idiots!**"

- The Spanish for **before** is **antes de.**   (ANTES DAY)
  Imagine it is your **auntie's day** before long.

- The Spanish for **empty** is **vacío.**   (VASEE O)
  Imagine thinking, "How can I **bathe you** if the
  bathtub is empty?"

- The Spanish for **occupied** (engaged) is   (OKOOPADO)
  ocupado.
  Imagine a bullfighter waiting before an
  occupied toilet.

☐ *You can write your answers in*

- What is the English for **ocupado**? _____

- What is the English for **vacío**? _____

- What is the English for **antes**? _____

- What is the English for **adiós**? _____

- What is the English for **hola**? _____

- What is the English for **perdone**? _____

- What is the English for **por favor**? _____

- What is the English for **gracias**? _____

← *Look back for the answers*

☐ *You can write your answers in*

- What is the Spanish for **occupied**? _____

- What is the Spanish for **empty**? _____

- What is the Spanish for **before**? _____

- What is the Spanish for **good-bye**? _____

- What is the Spanish for **hello**? _____

- What is the Spanish for **sorry**? _____

- What is the Spanish for **please**? _____

- What is the Spanish for **thank you**? _____

← *Look back for the answers*

□ Now cover up the answers below and translate the following:

□ *(You can write your answers in)*

1. Please, gentlemen, the pain is very bad.

2. My eyes and my skin are black.

3. Thank you, gentlemen, the hospital is always good.

4. Hello, I want a bandage before a dog.

5. Sorry, the telephone is not here.

_____

_____

_____

_____

_____

_____

_____

□ *The answers are:*

1. Por favor, señores, el dolor está muy malo.

2. Mis ojos y mi piel son negros.

3. Gracias, señores, el hospital es siempre bueno.

4. Hola, quiero una venda antes de un perro.

5. Perdone, el teléfono no está aquí.

☐ **Now cover up the answers below and translate the following:**

☐ *(You can write your answers in)*

1. Su cara es bonita, pero su vestido es viejo.

2. La mano está vacía.

3. La sangre está en el brazo y en la boca.

4. El ladrón quiere un fuego.

5. Es un accidente y una ambulancia está aquí.

_____

_____

_____

_____

_____

_____

_____

☐ *The answers are:*

1. Your (or his, her, its) face is pretty, but your (or his, her, its) dress is old.

2. The hand is empty.

3. The blood is on (or in) the arm and on (or in) the mouth.

4. The thief wants a fire.

5. It is an accident and an ambulance is here.

SOME MORE USEFUL VERBS

☐ **Think of each image in your mind's eye for about ten seconds**

- The Spanish for **I speak** is **hablo.**   (ABLO)
  Imagine when I *speak*, **I blow.**

- The Spanish for **I live** is **vivo.**   (VEEVO)
  Imagine I *live* like a **weevil.**

- The Spanish for **I sell** is **vendo.**   (VENDO)
  Imagine a street **vendor** who *sells* you
  something.

☐ *You can write your answers in*

- What is the English for **vendo**? _____

- What is the English for **vivo**? _____

- What is the English for **hablo**? _____

← *Look back for the answers*

☐ *You can write your answers in*

- What is the Spanish for **I sell**?   _____

- What is the Spanish for **I live**?   _____

- What is the Spanish for **I speak**?   _____

← *Look back for the answers*

ELEMENTARY GRAMMAR

Almost any adjective like *easy* or *quick* can be made into an adverb:

- *easily* or *quickly*

simply by adding *mente* (pronounced MENTAY) onto the end of the word in the feminine form.

➜ *So,*

- *He eats quickly* is *Come rápidamente*

- *I live quietly*   is *Vivo tranquilamente*

MONTHS OF THE YEAR

The next group of words consists of the months of the year.

• The Spanish for *January* is *enero* (pronounced ENERO).

Imagine months of Januaries *in a row.*

All of the other months sound reasonably like their English equivalents, so no "images" will be given to help remember them.

English	Spanish	Pronounced
January	enero	ENERO
February	febrero	FEBRERO
March	marzo	MARSO
April	abril	ABREEL
May	mayo	MAYO
June	junio	HOONEE O
July	julio	HOOLEE O
August	agosto	AGOSTO
September	septiembre	SETEE EMBRAY
October	octubre	OKTOOBRAY
November	noviembre	NOVEE EMBRAY
December	diciembre	DEESEE EMBRAY

☐ **Now cover up the answers below and translate the following:**

☐ *(You can write your answers in)*

1. I am ill today.

2. Good-bye; it is February; I am soon here.

3. The bathrooms are occupied.

4. I speak quietly; I live quietly; I sell telephones in March, in April, and in September.

5. He has a bad mouth and a bad cough.

_____

_____

_____

_____

_____

_____

☐ *The answers are:*

1. Estoy enfermo hoy.

2. Adiós; es febrero; estoy pronto aquí.

3. Los cuartos de baño están ocupados.

4. Hablo tranquilamente; vivo tranquilamente; vendo teléfonos en marzo, en abril y en septiembre.

5. Tiene una boca mala y un tos malo.

☐ **Now cover up the answers below and translate the following:**

☐ *(You can write your answers in)*

1. La muchacha y la mosca estaban muy enfermas en enero.

2. Vendo sillas, mesas y camas en mis tiendas.

3. Sí, está sucio, pero es muy caro.

4. Vendo muchas cebollas y mucha carne.

5. ¿Dónde está el perro hoy?

_____

_____

_____

_____

_____

_____

_____

☐ *The answers are:*

1. The girl and the fly were very ill in January.

2. I sell chairs, tables, and beds in my shops.

3. Yes, it is dirty, but it is very expensive.

4. I sell many onions and much meat. (*Mucho* in the plural—*muchos* or *muchas*—means *many*.)

5. Where is the dog today?

A NUMBER OF USEFUL WORDS

☐ **Think of each image in your mind's eye for about ten seconds**

- The Spanish for **glasses** (spectacles) is (las) **gafas**.   (GAFAS)
  Imagine an Irishman saying, "**Give us** my glasses."

- The Spanish for **left** is **izquierdo**.   (EESKEE ERDO)
  Imagine thinking the driver in front is scared o'
  turning left.

- The Spanish for **right** is **derecho**.   (DERECHO)
  Imagine asking if turning right will lead you in
  the correct **direction**.

- The Spanish for **enough** is **bastante**.   (BASTANTAY)
  Imagine thinking, "You've **passed auntie**
  enough sweets."

- The Spanish for **serious** is **grave**.   (GRAVAY)
  Imagine feeling **grave** and serious.

- The Spanish for **town** is (la) **ciudad**.   (SEE OODAD)
  Imagine pointing to a town and saying, "I'll **see**
  your Dad."

- The Spanish for **butter** is **mantequilla**.   (MANTEKEELYA)
  Imagine you hire a **man to kill a** rat that
  steals your butter.

- The Spanish for **tart** is **tarta**.   (TARTA)
  Imagine a bullfighter eating a **tart**.

- The Spanish for **grape** is **uva**.   (OOVA)
  Imagine someone saying, "**You have a**
  grape."

- The Spanish for **salad** is **ensalada**.   (ENSALADA)
  Imagine being covered **in salad**.

☐ *You can write your answers in*

- What is the English for **ensalada**? _____

- What is the English for **uva**? _____

- What is the English for **tarta**? _____

- What is the English for **mantequilla**? _____

- What is the English for **ciudad**? _____

- What is the English for **grave**? _____

- What is the English for **bastante**? _____

- What is the English for **derecho**? _____

- What is the English for **izquierdo**? _____

- What is the English for (las) **gafas**? _____

← *Look back for the answers*

☐ *You can write your answers in*

- What is the Spanish for **salad**?   _____

- What is the Spanish for **grape**?   _____

- What is the Spanish for **tart**?   _____

- What is the Spanish for **butter**?   _____

- What is the Spanish for **town**?   _____

- What is the Spanish for **serious**?   _____

- What is the Spanish for **enough**?   _____

- What is the Spanish for **right**?   _____

- What is the Spanish for **left**?   _____

- What is the Spanish for **glasses**?   _____

← *Look back for the answers*

SOME MORE USEFUL WORDS

☐ **Think of each image in your mind's eye for about ten seconds**

- The Spanish for **cigarette** is **cigarillo.** (SEEGAREELYO)
  Imagine Spanish cigarettes are like little
  cigars that make you **ill oh!**

- The Spanish for **breakfast** is **desayuno.** (DESAYOONO)
  Imagine someone coming up to you in a hotel
  and saying, "**They say you know** when
  breakfast is."

- The Spanish for **lunch** is **comida.** (KOMEEDA)
  Imagine lunch in your hotel is a complete
  comedy of errors.

- The Spanish for **dinner** is **cena.** (SENA)
  Imagine being **sane** while eating your dinner.

- The Spanish for **tip** is **propina.** (PROPEENA)
  Imagine **propping** up a cup with your waiter's tip.

- The Spanish for **tourist** is (el) **turista.** (TOOREESTA)
  Imagine a bullfighter talking to a group of
  tourists.

- The Spanish for **tobacco** is **tabaco.** (TABAKO)
  Imagine a bullfighter filling his pipe with **tobacco.**

- The Spanish for **newspaper** is **periódico.** (PEREE ODEEKO)
  Imagine looking at your newspaper **periodically.**

- The Spanish for **name** is **nombre.** (NOMBRAY)
  Imagine asking a policeman for his name and
  number.

- The Spanish for **soap** is **jabón.** (HABON)
  Imagine giving a child a piece of soap and
  saying, "**Have one.**"

- What is the English for **jabón**? _____

- What is the English for **nombre**? _____

- What is the English for **periódico**? _____

- What is the English for **tabaco**? _____

- What is the English for (el) **turista**? _____

- What is the English for **propina**? _____

- What is the English for **cena**? _____

- What is the English for **comida**? _____

- What is the English for **desayuno**? _____

- What is the English for **cigarillo**? _____

← *Look back for the answers*

☐ *You can write your answers in*

- What is the Spanish for **soap**?   _____

- What is the Spanish for **name**?   _____

- What is the Spanish for **newspaper**?   _____

- What is the Spanish for **tobacco**?   _____

- What is the Spanish for **tourist**?   _____

- What is the Spanish for **tip**?   _____

- What is the Spanish for **dinner**?   _____

- What is the Spanish for **lunch**?   _____

- What is the Spanish for **breakfast**?   _____

- What is the Spanish for **cigarette**?   _____

← *Look back for the answers*

AND FINALLY, SOME MORE USEFUL WORDS

☐ **Think of each image in your mind's eye for about ten seconds**

- The Spanish for **I give** is **doy.**   (DOY)
  Imagine thinking that I must *give* my brother a
  toy for his birthday.

- The Spanish for **I put** is **pongo.**   (PONGO)
  Imagine thinking "If I *put* the paint here, it will
  make the **pond go** green."

- The Spanish for **I go** is **voy.**   (VOY)
  Imagine thinking "I *go* on a **voy**age."

☐ *You can write your answers in*

- What is the English for **voy**?   _____

- What is the English for **pongo**?   _____

- What is the English for **doy**?   _____

← *Look back for the answers*

☐ *You can write your answers in*

- What is the Spanish for **I go**?   _____

- What is the Spanish for **I put**?   _____

- What is the Spanish for **I give**?   _____

← *Look back for the answers*

243

□ **Now cover up the answers below and translate the following:**

□ *(You can write your answers in)*

1. I put the glasses, the butter, and the tart on the newspaper.

2. I give the soap today.

3. I eat the breakfast, the salad, and the lunch, and I eat the dinner.

4. I am going there, and the tourist is in the street.

5. I want the soap and the tobacco, but I do not want cigarettes and I do not want a tip.

_____

_____

_____

_____

_____

_____

□ *The answers are:*

1. Pongo las gafas, la mantequilla y la tarta en el periódico.

2. Doy el jabón hoy.

3. Como el desayuno, la ensalada y la comida, y como la cena.

4. Voy allá, y el turista está en la calle.

5. Quiero el jabón y el tabaco, pero no quiero cigarillos y no quiero propina.

☐ Now cover up the answers below and translate the following:

☐ *(You can write your answers in)*

1. El nombre está en la mantequilla y en la ciudad.

2. Estoy tranquilo. Es octubre y la uva está en la tarta.

3. No es noviembre. No es diciembre. No es agosto. Es enero.

4. Vendo el periódico en mayo, junio y julio.

5. No quiero el jabón.

_____

_____

_____

_____

_____

_____

_____

☐ *The answers are:*

1. The name is on (*or* in) the butter and in the town.

2. I am quiet. It is October and the grape is in the tart.

3. It is not November. It is not December. It is not August. It is January.

4. I sell the newspaper in May, June, and July.

5. I do not want the soap.

This is the end of the course. We hope you have enjoyed it! Of course words and grammar will not be remembered forever without review, but if you look at the book from time to time, you will be surprised at how quickly everything comes back.

When you go abroad, do not be too shy to try out what you have learned. Your host will appreciate your making the effort to speak, even if you make mistakes. And the more you attempt to speak, the more you will learn!

GLOSSARY

a (an)	un/una	brother	hermano
accident	accidente	bull	toro
accountant	(el) contador	bullfight	corrida
afternoon	(la) tarde	bus	(el) autobús
always	siempre	business	negocio
am	estoy/soy	but	pero
ambulance	ambulancia	butter	mantequilla
and	y	cabbage	(la) col
angry	enojado	cake	(el) pastel
animal	animal	camping site	(el) camping
are	son/están	car	carro
arm	brazo	cat	gato
bad	malo	cauliflower	(la) coliflor
bandage	venda	chair	silla
bank	banco	cheap	barato
barber's shop	barbería	check	(el) cheque
bath	baño	cheese	queso
bathroom	cuarto de baño	chicken	pollo
bathing trunks	(el) bañador	cigarette	cigarillo
beach	playa	cloakroom	(el) guardarropa
bear	oso	clock	(el) reloj
bed	cama	coat	abrigo
bedroom	dormitorio	coffee	(el) café
bee	abeja	cold	frío
beer	cerveza	color	(el) color
before	antes	cough	(la) tos
bill	cuenta	cow	vaca
bird	pájaro	cup	taza
black	negro	cupboard	armario
blood	(la) sangre	curtain	cortina
blouse	blusa	customs	aduana
blue	azul	danger	peligro
boat	barco	daughter	hija
book	libro	day	(el) día
boss	(el) jefe	dead	muerto
bottle	botella	deck chair	hamaca
boy	muchacho	deep	profundo
bread	(el) pan	dentist	(el) dentista
breakfast	desayuno	dining room	(el) comedor

dinner	cena	garden	(el) jardín
dirty	sucio	gasoline	gasolina
doctor	médico	gentlemen	(los) señores
dog	perro	girl	muchacha
donkey	burro	glasses	(las) gafas
door	puerta	goat	cabra
drawer	(el) cajón	good	bueno
dress	vestido	good-bye	adiós
driver	(el) conductor	goose	ganso
duck	pato	grape	uva
easy	fácil	gray	gris
eat (eats)	come	green	verde
eat (they)	comen	hand	(la) mano
egg	huevo	hard	duro
empty	vacío	hardware store	ferretería
engine	(el) motor	hat	sombrero
enough	bastante	have (has)	tiene
entrance	entrada	have (they)	tienen
envelope	(el) sobre	heat	(el) calor
exhaust	(el) escape	hello	hola
exit	salida	help	ayuda
expensive	caro	her	su/sus
eye	ojo	here	aquí
face	cara	high	alto
factory	fábrica	his	su/sus
fan	(el) ventilador	holidays	(las) vacaciones
father	(el) padre	(vacation)	
fire	fuego	horse	caballo
first	primero	hospital	(el) hospital
fish	(el) pez	hotel	(el) hotel
flat tire	pinchazo	hour	hora
floor	suelo	how	cómo
flower	(la) flor	how much	cuánto
fly	mosca	husband	marido
fork	(el) tenedor	I eat	como
free	libre	I give	doy
fresh	fresco	I go	voy
friend	amigo	I have	tengo
frog	rana	I live	vivo
fruit	fruta	I make	hago
garage	(el) garaje	I put	pongo

I sell	vendo	mouse	(el) ratón
I speak	hablo	mouth	boca
I want	quiero	much	mucho
ill	enfermo	museum	museo
in	en	mushroom	seta
is	está/es	my	mi/mis
its	su/sus	name	(el) nombre
jack	gato	newspaper	periódico
jellyfish	medusa	night	(la) noche
job	empleo	no/not	no
key	(la) llave	number	número
kitchen	cocina	occupied	ocupado
knife	cuchillo	office	oficina
ladies	señoras	oil	(el) aceite
lake	lago	old	viejo
last	último	on	en
laundromat	lavandería	onion	cebolla
lawyer	abogado	only	solamente
left	izquierdo	or	o
less	menos	outside	fuera de
letter	carta	owner	propietario
little	pequeño	pain	(el) dolor
long	largo	paper	(el) papel
lunch	comida	party	fiesta
mail box	(el) buzón	passport	(el) pasaporte
manager	director	path	senda
map	(el) mapa	pear	pera
market	mercado	pen	pluma
meat	(la) carne	pharmacy	farmacia
menu	menú	piano	piano
milk	(la) leche	picnic	merienda
minute	minuto	pig	puerco
mirror	espejo	plant	planta
mistake	(el) error	plate	plato
money	dinero	please	por favor
monkey	mono	police	policía
month	(el) mes	post office	correo
more	más	potato	papa
morning	mañana	pretty	bonito
mother	(la) madre	price	precio
mountain	montaña	product	producto

pump	bomba	soup	sopa
quick	rápido	stairs	escalera
quickly	rápidamente	stamp	sello
quiet	tranquilo	storm	tormenta
quietly	tranquilamente	sugar	(el) azúcar
rat	rata	suitcase	maleta
receipt	recibo	sun	(el) sol
receptionist	recepcionista	supermarket	supermercado
red	rojo	table	mesa
rescue (to)	salvar	tablecloth	(el) mantel
restaurant	(el) restaurante	tank (gas)	depósito
rice	(el) arroz	tart	tarta
right (correct)	correcto	telephone	teléfono
right	derecho	thank you	gracias
river	río	the (plural)	los/las
road	carretera	the	el/la
rock	roca	there	allá
room	(la) habitación	thief	ladrón
salad	ensalada	thing	cosa
salary	salario	ticket	(el) billete
salesperson	(el) vendedor	time	tiempo
salmon	(el) salmón	tip	propina
sand	arena	tire	neumático
sea	(el) mar	tobacco	tabaco
seat	asiento	tobacco shop	tabaquería
second (adj.)	segundo	today	hoy
second	segundo	tomato	(el) tomate
serious	grave	tourist	(el) turista
shelf	(el) estante	town	(la) ciudad
shirt	camisa	train	(el) tren
shoe	zapato	tree	(el) árbol
shop	tienda	trousers	(los) pantalones
sir	(el) señor	(pants)	
sister	hermana	under	debajo de
skin	(la) piel	vacation	(las) vacaciones
skirt	falda	very	muy
soap	(el) jabón	waitress	camarera
some	unos/unas	wall	(la) pared
son	hijo	want (they)	quieren
soon	pronto	want (wants)	quiere
sorry	perdone	was	estaba

wasp	avispa	**Numbers**	
week	semana	zero	cero
were	estaban	one	uno
wheel	rueda	two	dos
where	dónde	three	tres
white	blanco	four	cuatro
who	quién	five	cinco
why	por qué	six	seis
wife	mujer	seven	siete
window	ventana	eight	ocho
wine	vino	nine	nueve
wrong	incorrecto	ten	diez
year	año	eleven	once
yellow	amarillo	twelve	doce
yes	sí	twenty	veinte
yesterday	ayer	twenty-five	veinticinco
your	su/sus	quarter	cuarto
		half	media

Days of the Week

Monday	lunes
Tuesday	martes
Wednesday	miércoles
Thursday	jueves
Friday	viernes
Saturday	sábado
Sunday	domingo

Months of the Year

January	enero
February	febrero
March	marzo
April	abril
May	mayo
June	junio
July	julio
August	agosto
September	septiembre
October	octubre
November	noviembre
December	diciembre